Surviving Childhood Sexual Abuse Workbook

Surviving Childhood Sexual Abuse Workbook

Practical exercises for
working on problems
resulting from childhood abuse

Carolyn Ainscough
Kay Toon

DA CAPO PRESS
A Member of the Perseus Books Group

North American edition © 2000 by Da Capo Press
Copyright © 2000 by Carolyn Ainscough and Kay Toon

First published in Great Britain in 2000 by Society for Promoting Christian Knowledge, Holy Trinity Church, Marylebone Road, London NWI 4DU.

ISBN-10: 1-55561-290-3   ISBN-13: 978-1-55561-290-0

Text design by Rachel Hegarty
Set in 11-point Palatino by Perseus Publishing Services

Da Capo Press is a member of the Perseus Books Group.
Find us on the World Wide Web at http://www.dacapopress.com
Da Capo Press books are available at special discounts for bulk purchases in the United States by corporations, institutions, and other organizations.

Contents

Preface

Surviving Childhood Sexual Abuse Workbook is for male and female adult survivors of childhood sexual abuse (referred to in this book as "survivors"). This resource guides you step-by-step through a series of exercises aimed at recognizing, understanding and working on the problems resulting from childhood abuse. The workbook is a companion to *Surviving Childhood Sexual Abuse: Practical Self-Help for Adults Who Were Sexually Abused as Children, Revised Edition* (Fisher Books, 2000).

Since *Surviving Childhood Sexual Abuse* was first published, we have continued to work with adult survivors of childhood sexual abuse referred to the clinic where we have worked for many years. We also work outside the health services, providing training and consultations to people who work with survivors of childhood sexual abuse. We have received feedback from many survivors describing how *Surviving Childhood Sexual Abuse* has helped them understand more about sexual abuse and encouraged them to work on their problems by themselves or with professional support. Therapists have also told us that they found the book useful when working with survivors.

Many people have told us they wanted to know more on a practical level about how to overcome the problems resulting from sexual abuse and about the difficulties that are often encountered. We wrote the workbook as a practical guide primarily for survivors. We also hope therapists will find these exercises useful for working with survivors individually or in groups. Many survivors have contributed their own completed exercises to this book and have also written about their experiences of doing the exercises. We hope this helps to give a fuller picture of the healing process—the struggles and the setbacks, as well as what helps survivors cope and move on.

Although public awareness of child abuse has increased in recent years, much remains to be done to prevent child abuse and to help adult survivors who are still suffering. We hope this workbook will help contribute to survivors taking control of their lives, feeling more confident and fulfilling their potential. We continue to believe in the powerful effects of breaking the silence about child abuse and to feel inspired by survivors' strength to heal and to grow.

Acknowledgements

The exercises in this book developed over a number of years from our work with survivors in our clinic and we would like to thank all those survivors for sharing their experiences and for inspiring us with their courage. We particularly want to thank the survivors who over the last year completed draft exercises, gave suggestions and comments and generously contributed their writings to this book. We would also like to thank survivors from the support network Moving On for their many contributions and for their constant enthusiasm and encouragement. Thanks to Leslie Cohen, Jon Fraise and Sue Richardson for their comments on the Introduction and to Mary Penford for providing illustrations for the chapter on mothers.   —*Carolyn Ainscough and Kay Toon*

Many friends have helped during the writing of this book, and I would like to thank the following people for giving their time and supporting me by reading through the many drafts of the book, for feeding back helpful suggestions and for their encouragement: Chris Bethlehem, Em Edmondson, Diane Skinner and James Taylor. Writing a book inevitably takes time away from families and friends and I would like especially to thank Jerry Hardman-Jones, Kirstie, Catriona, John and Tag, for their patience and support throughout the development of this book.   —*Kay Toon*

My thanks to Margaret Ainscough, Andrew Lister and Mandy McFarlane for reading through draft chapters and for their thoughtful comments.

—*Carolyn Ainscough*

Introduction

I have walked through the valley of the shadow of death and emerged into sunlight, stronger. I am no longer an empty shell. I look forward to living every day. There is joy in the simple things of life. Fear no longer grips me. I feel that I am able to breathe and that I have a right to live.   —*Calli*

Millions of people are survivors of childhood sexual abuse, and now more and more are speaking out and finding ways to break free from their past. In our previous book, *Surviving Childhood Sexual Abuse, Revised Edition* (Fisher Books), many survivors who came to our clinic spoke up about what had happened to them. We know that their courage has helped other survivors face their own past and take the first steps toward a better future. *Surviving Childhood Sexual Abuse Workbook* draws on background information from *Surviving Childhood Sexual Abuse* and is a companion to that book. It employs practical, step-by-step exercises for working on problems that result from being sexually abused as a child. The two books may be used separately or together.

Many survivors have completed these exercises and contributed their writings and experiences to this book. The exercises are designed to help you think in a new way about your past, gradually break free from the problems that are disrupting your life and look forward to your future.

Is This Book for Me?

This book is for male and female survivors of childhood sexual abuse who want to explore the effects of their experiences and to work on their current difficulties. Sexual abuse is any kind of sexual behavior by an adult with a child, or any unwanted or inappropriate sexual behavior from another child. Your abuser may have been a man or a woman; you may have been abused by one person, many different individuals or you may have been abused by a group of people. You will find more information about what sexual abuse is and the terms we use in this book at the end of this chapter.

Being sexually abused as a child affects people to differing degrees. How you have been affected will depend on a number of factors, including who abused you; how long the abuse went on; how old you were when it started and ended (or it may be ongoing); what was done and said to you; and if you had any good experiences, support or care in your childhood. Some survivors will be able to come to terms with what has happened to them by themselves, by seeking support and help from family and friends, or by using this self-help workbook. Some survivors may also need to seek professional help from a therapist or mental health worker. Every survivor's experience is unique, and each survivor will need different levels of help and support.

The exercises in this book can be painful at times, but they can also be beneficial. However, they need to be used with caution because they can stir up strong feelings and have powerful effects. Your safety and well-being are of the utmost importance, and you need to think about what level of support you require.

- You can use this book on your own, but we recommend that you think about sources of support before you start (see chapter 1).
- If you are already receiving counseling, psychological or psychiatric help or are taking medication for psychological problems, we advise you to speak to your therapist or doctor before embarking on these exercises. Your therapist or counselor may be happy to work through this book with you.
- If you have severe problems or engage in life-threatening behavior, such as serious self-harm, only use this book with the help of a professional mental health worker.

We know that many survivors can be helped by these exercises, but we do not pretend to have magical answers to your problems. It is possible to break free from the damaging effects of sexual abuse but this can take time. You may have had problems over many years and they won't just disappear overnight. This book is not intended as a substitute for professional help—in fact, we hope that completing this workbook might encourage some of you to seek further help. Many of the exercises in this book are also useful for people who have been physically or emotionally abused as children.

About This Book

This book focuses on practical ways to identify and change harmful beliefs and behaviors resulting from being sexually abused as a child. It also aims to help you work through your feelings about the abuse and feel better about yourself. In each chapter are exercises for you to do, plus charts and checklists to fill in. The exercises are presented in a step-by-step format, with each exercise building on what was done in the previous exercise. You will find space in the book to complete the exercises so you can build a personal record of your journey toward healing. We include examples of the exercises completed by both male and female survivors. Survivors also comment in these pages on the benefits and difficulties of these exercises and what helped them cope.

Part 1. Beginnings:
Understanding Your Present Problems and Keeping Safe

Chapter 1 looks at how to keep safe while using this book. Be sure to read this chapter first because it will help you prepare for difficulties that might arise. This chapter will help you evaluate your possible sources of support and tell you how to take care of yourself while you are doing the exercises. Chapter 2 begins the process of helping you face your own past experiences. The exercises help you link past experiences to present problems. Chapter 3 helps you to become aware of the coping strategies that you use currently and to move to consciously using nonharmful coping strategies. Chapter 4 helps you identify and deal with the things that trigger extreme feelings and behaviors, flashbacks and hallucinations.

Part 2. Guilt and Self-Blame

Chapters 5, 6 and 7 are about the feelings of guilt and self-blame that survivors so often experience. Many survivors believe they are responsible for being abused because they didn't stop the abuse or didn't tell anyone, or because they think they caused the abuse to happen. The exercises in these chapters help you to challenge these kinds of beliefs and to understand that the responsibility for abuse always lies with the abuser and never with the abused child.

Part 3. Feelings about Yourself and Others

Chapter 8 ("Abusers") is about exploring your feelings toward your abuser(s) and regaining your own power. Chapter 9 ("Mothers and Other

Principal Caregivers") contains exercises to help you explore your feelings about your mother (or any other person close to you who didn't sexually abuse you as a child and should have protected you). Chapter 10 (Childhood) helps you to look back on yourself as a child, and to communicate with and nurture the child you were. It also helps you understand why you might have difficulties relating to children.

Part 4. Looking toward the Future

Chapter 11 helps you assess the progress you have made so far and to look at what further steps you might want to take in the future.

This book is a first step toward healing, rather than a final solution. We hope it will give you the confidence to break free of your past by sharing your experiences with others, contacting other survivors of sexual abuse and going for professional help. The resources section at the end of the book gives details about where you can seek further help.

Is This the Right Time to Use This Workbook?

When is the right time to work on your abuse experience(s)? Many survivors are frightened about the consequences of working on their abuse. This is understandable. Doing anything different is a risk. If you have coped in the past by trying to forget about your abuse, doing these exercises is a radically different approach, and it will take a leap of faith to get started. The exercise below will help you examine what is standing in your way, preventing you from getting started. It will also help you to decide if now is the right time for you to start this workbook.

EXERCISE 1 IS THIS THE RIGHT TIME?

Purpose To help you think about whether this is the right time to start using this workbook and to understand more about what might be stopping you from looking at the abuse and working on your difficulties.

Below are a number of reasons given by survivors for not starting to work on their past abuse and current difficulties. Check any reasons that apply to you, and add any others you can think of below.

Current situation:	Applies to you?
In school	_____
Relationship break-up	_____

Current situation: **Applies to you?**

    Pregnant   _____

    Just started a new job   _____

    Just started a new relationship   _____

Fear of:

    What you might feel   _____

    What you might remember   _____

    Not being able to cope   _____

    What your family/partner/friends will think _____

    The consequences of beginning to change _____

    Being hurt or rejected   _____

When you are feeling depressed or anxious, saying to yourself:

    I'm depressed and I don't want
      to make things worse   _____

    I'm depressed and I don't have
      the resources to cope   _____

When you are feeling OK, saying to yourself:

    I'm OK and I don't want to risk making
      myself depressed again   _____

    I'm OK and everything is figured out now _____

Thinking (or being told):

    You should look forward rather than
      dwell on the past   _____

    You are making a mountain
      out of a molehill   _____

    Your experiences and problems
      are too big to figure out   _____

    Your problems will go away
      by themselves   _____

Too busy—putting other things or other people first _____

Being unsure whether your memories are of real events _____

> **Survivor's comment**
>
> The exercises need to be carried out when you are ready to face issues; otherwise, there is minimal progress. It is about daring to believe the truth and step by step becoming stronger in that belief. —*Calli*

Current situation

If you are in a particular crisis at the moment or have to deal with something very important right now, you may want to wait until you feel more stable or have more space and time to cope with doing this work.

> I think the right time to do these exercises is when you are out of the abusive situation with a safe place to live, and you become aware that there is a recurrent problem that you want to try to solve. —*Catherine*

> I think it could be the wrong time to do the exercises if you are feeling extremely stressed or uncomfortable. It may mean you have to do them in small portions, but at least you will be doing them from a position of strength, which is always best. —*Rebecca*

> Everyone is individual, but I think you need to be ready to do the exercises. I think it is difficult if your present-day situation is in turmoil—for example, marriage breakup, loss and grief, or if you have no outside support. —*Sarah*

If you do not feel ready to work on the exercises right now, you may feel able to read *Surviving Childhood Sexual Abuse* now and return to this workbook later.

It Might Be Painful

Many people try to cope with sexual abuse by blocking their memories and feelings. This is one of the few ways in which children are able to cope, but this strategy has disadvantages. It doesn't work completely and it doesn't last. Bad feelings and memories "escape" as nightmares, panic attacks, fears, depression, sexual difficulties, flashbacks and many other problems. These problems are the symptoms of the underlying trauma of being sexually abused. It can be difficult to get rid of the symptoms until the underlying problem is dealt with.

Working on your past experiences and current problems is not easy. It will probably bring up feelings and memories that are painful and hard to cope with. However, you would probably not be reading this book if you were totally happy with the way things are for you at the moment. Working on yourself can be hard, but it is also very rewarding. Many survivors feel that by working on themselves they become more aware of who they are and what they want, and they begin to see a way through their problems.

I'm OK/I'm Depressed

Many survivors alternate between feeling reasonably OK and having bouts of depression or anxiety or even feeling suicidal. When you are feeling OK, understandably you want to believe that your problems have gone away and will not come back. Although people can often block their feelings and memories for a time and feel OK, they cannot do this all the time—and then they experience another period of depression or anxiety. Look back over the last few years of your life and see if you recognize this pattern. Working on your abuse will mean facing painful feelings, but it can also help you stop this pattern of plunging in and out of periods of extreme emotions.

It's in the Past

Survivors are often told, "It's in the past, forget about it." Friends and family who hear you talking about the abuse or see your distress may feel uncomfortable and not know what to do or how to respond. Saying "forget about it" might be a way of refusing to get involved, or it might be a genuine attempt to be helpful. It isn't. Unfortunately, doctors and health workers also sometimes give this unhelpful advice. You may have also said this to yourself. If you could forget about the past and not be affected by it, you would. No one wants to dwell on unhappy events or create problems just for the sake of it. Past events need to be brought into full awareness, understood and processed before we can truly let go of them and move on.

If you remember and relive the hurt and pain you went through, it will help you put it in the back of your mind and help you start to live a normal life. I thought the idea was to try to forget, but I realize now that I will never forget what they did to me. I don't want to forget, I want to understand and come to terms with it.   —Jean

I'm Making a Mountain out of a Molehill

The sexual abuse of a child is a serious crime and a trauma that should not have to be endured. It is normal to experience difficulties when you have been traumatized. Trying to face your difficulties and deal with them is a courageous act. It isn't whining and making a fuss about nothing.

What Will Other People Think?

You cannot control what other people will think and feel about your decision to work on your abuse. Some people will be supportive, but others may be hostile. Sometimes people do not understand what effects the abuse can have. They may think that you are getting worse if you cry or get angry. They may want to try and stop you from continuing with these exercises because they are trying to protect you or because they feel it would be easier for them if you remained silent about what has happened.

It is normal to feel angry and upset about being abused, and you have a right to express your feelings and speak up about what has happened to you if you want to. During the abuse your feelings were ignored and you had to remain silent. Now you have a chance to begin to undo the wrongs that were done to you.

Did It Really Happen?

Sometimes survivors wonder whether the abuse really happened or whether they are imagining it. This can be a bigger problem if

- You do not have complete memories.
- You blocked memories of the abuse for a period of time and now have access to them again.
- Your memories and feelings are surfacing in flashbacks and dreams.
- You were in a confused state of mind during the abuse because you were half asleep or intoxicated with alcohol or drugs or did not really understand what was happening.
- Your abuser has denied the abuse.
- Your abuser was also warm and caring.
- Other people have not believed you.
- You have read about people having so-called "false memory syndrome."

- You coped with the abuse as a child by pretending it was a dream or that it was happening to someone else.
- What you remember seems too extreme or bizarre to be true.

Many survivors have these worries and difficulties. Pretending the abuse didn't happen and blocking painful memories and feelings is a common way of coping with any trauma and can leave people feeling confused about what really happened. Some survivors say they have lost access to all memories of their abuse for periods of time, even when there is concrete evidence about what has happened to them. Memories of the past can be triggered by current events, such as a baby's birth or the death of an abuser. Memories of frightening events may also be accessed again when you begin to feel safe or strong enough to deal with them.

If you do not have full memories, you may be anxious to find out what happened to you; however, this is not something that can be forced. Survivors often gain access to memories gradually, and this helps to protect them from becoming overwhelmed. Memories can also become distorted over time and some survivors may never know for sure exactly what happened to them. However, you do not need to have full and exact memories to use this workbook. Doing these exercises can help you explore your feelings and beliefs and develop a new understanding of yourself and your experiences.

Some people have no memories of abuse but suffer from symptoms and problems that make them wonder whether they have been abused. It is not possible to "diagnose" a past history of sexual abuse from current problems and symptoms, and this book cannot tell you whether you have been sexually abused. If you have no memories of abuse but have symptoms and difficulties you wish to deal with, it is advisable to consult a therapist rather than using this book.

Writing

Every chapter contains exercises that ask you to write about your feelings and experiences. Many survivors find that writing plays an important part in their recovery. Some survivors find the idea of writing threatening and may also feel that it won't be helpful. Writing can make the reality of what has happened clear. Although this process can be frightening, it can also be healing.

Writing made me face up to the reality of the abuse. It helped me acknowledge the abuse instead of trying to lock it up. I could no longer deny it. I was frightened but it does get better. It was worth it in the end. —*Maya*

Writing isn't the same as just thinking things out. Many survivors recall memories and feelings and begin to understand themselves better once they begin to write.

You may feel anxious about writing and feel you will fail or not do a "good job." The education of many survivors has suffered because of abuse during childhood. You may have been punished, laughed at or called stupid. Try to remember that you are not being tested on your writing. The writing is for you, to help you gain access to your thoughts and feelings. Spelling, grammar and style don't matter.

Alternative Ways to Complete the Exercises

There are many ways of responding in the exercises. You don't have to write "essay style." You could write a list, or write down key words. You could make a chart or a diagram. Many survivors enjoy writing poetry—you could complete the exercises in poems. Do whatever feels easiest and most comfortable. If you have trouble writing, you might speak into a tape recorder, get someone you trust to write as you speak, or use one of the alternatives to writing described below.

The writing is for *your* benefit. No one else has to read it. If you are worried that someone else might find your writing, keep it in a safe place or leave it in a sealed envelope with someone you trust. Writing can also be a good way of communicating your experiences and feelings to other people without having to talk, so you may want to share your writing with someone else. Sharing your writing also helps to break the secrecy of your abuse.

Keep a daily diary of what you do in your life—even little things, especially if they are positive. This will

- Provide you with an outline of your experiences.
- Show your progress.
- Remind you of how brave you have been.
- Remind you of positive and happy things that have happened to you.

- Be a record of an important part of your life and development as a person.

It is important to date all your writings and keep them somewhere safe. I find this really helps me see how I am progressing and pulls experiences together that might be forgotten otherwise. Also record your dreams—they can be very significant in suggesting you are making progress on a deeper level.   —*Annabelle*

I was so programmed into a "don't tell or else" dogma that I thought I would suffer a fate worse than death if I wrote things down. Luckily I had a very supportive counselor who let me work on the writing during our sessions and helped allay my fears. I took it step by step until I gained confidence and became angry about the abuse. I have found my own personal power now and it is a good feeling to know that I can write and that this is a valuable resource. As you can see, I am not frightened of writing anymore.   —*Maya*

The exercises have gotten me to write, which I've always avoided. Before, when I thought about the past, I pushed it aside. Now I think I don't have to bury it deep in my head. I'm writing it down and finding that helpful. It's one way of getting it out of my system, although it hurts. I never wanted to read in black and white what my abuser did, but now I'm beginning to realize that the only way I can do something about my problems is by recognizing what he did and fighting back. By writing it down, you can break the hold he has on you. Now I want to write and write and write. The more I write, the easier it gets. I feel like I am never going to stop. There is so much to write and get out of my system.   —*Jean*

Alternatives to Writing

Not everyone feels comfortable with writing. In some of the exercises in the book we have suggested alternatives to writing. You could also try to adapt the other exercises and use one of the methods below.

Drawing, Painting, Using Art Materials

When you are asked to write about an event or about how you feel, you may be happier drawing, painting or using art materials instead. You could draw stick figures or a sequence of events like a cartoon. You could use clay or salt-flour dough to sculpt objects or scenes. Some survivors we know have made collages to represent their answers to the exercises. Painting can be a powerful way of expressing your feelings. Color can be used to represent different feelings, different people or different times of your life. You do not have to be artistic in any way to use these methods. The aim is not to create a work of art but to find a different way of expressing your thoughts and feelings and getting in touch with ideas and feelings you may not be consciously aware of.

Talking

If you find talking is easier than writing, you could talk through the exercises with another person or use the technique of talking to an empty chair. Sit in a chair with an empty chair opposite you and imagine that another person is sitting on that chair. This "other person" could be someone you know and trust, an imaginary safe person or a part of yourself. Talk through the exercises with this person. Talk out loud rather than in your head. You could try talking through the exercises as a first step toward writing.

The Words We Use

Sexual Abuse

We use the term "sexual abuse" to mean any kind of sexual behavior by an adult with a child or any unwanted or inappropriate sexual behavior from another child. This includes sexual intercourse, oral sex, anal sex, being touched in a sexual way and being persuaded to touch someone else. It may involve inserting objects into the child's body or sexual acts with animals. However, sexual abuse doesn't always involve physical contact. Being made to watch other people's sexual behavior, or to look at their bodies or at sexual photographs or videos can also be forms of sexual abuse. Sexual abuse includes abuse by one person, abuse by a number of different people or by groups of people. The abuse may have happened only once or many times over a number of years. It may still be happening now.

Abusers

An abuser is anyone who has sexually abused a child. This could be a father, mother, brother, other family member, friend, person in authority, acquaintance, older child or a stranger. Although the majority of abusers are thought to be men (maybe 80 percent), many survivors have been abused by women.

Child

The word "child" is used here to refer to teenagers as well as younger children. Abuse can start as a teenager or in adulthood. This book is primarily for people whose sexual abuse started before they became adults.

Survivors

We use the word "survivors" to refer to men and women who have been sexually abused as children. They have had to find ways of surviving the trauma of sexual abuse but, with the help of this book, we hope they will go beyond simply surviving to living a fuller and happier life.

Survivors and abusers can come from any walk of life and any religious or ethnic background.

Many survivors have contributed their writings to this book to share with you their struggles, their experiences, their hopes and their successes.

> The chaos in my head was too big to handle on my own. I needed help to break it down so I could work it out. To try to think things through yourself is daunting. The exercises managed to organize my thoughts into smaller parts so I could consider them more thoroughly. I also need prompting before I think about my abuse—the exercises provided that prompt. I am now more positive and able to communicate. The exercises have helped me to feel more self-confident and in control of my life.
> —Catherine

This book does not contain all the answers to your problems, but it could be a first step toward breaking free of your past and beginning to move on. Now make sure you turn to the next chapter, which gives advice on how to use the workbook and how to keep safe while doing the exercises. Good luck with the work ahead!

PART I

Beginnings

Understanding Your Current Problems
and Keeping Safe

This section is provided to help you understand more about how the abuse has affected your life and to provide ways of coping and feeling safe. Chapter 2 helps you focus on your current problems and explains how sexual abuse can lead to problems. Chapters 1, 3 and 4 discuss how to learn to feel safe and how to deal with difficult feelings, memories and symptoms.

1

How to Use This Book and Keep Safe

This chapter suggests how to do the exercises in this book and helps you find ways of feeling safe while doing them. The exercises are designed to help you challenge your beliefs, reassess your past and process your feelings. Working on your thoughts and feelings about the past can be very distressing, so it is important for you to maintain some control over how deeply you get into your feelings. As a child, you were treated as though your feelings did not matter. The sexual abuse was to satisfy the desires of the abuser; how you felt was not important to him or her. You *are* important and it *does* matter how you feel.

It is important that you take care of yourself while you do these exercises, that you move through them at your own pace and that you feel in control of what you are going through. This chapter looks at what you need to know before you start the exercises, how to protect yourself and create the right emotional distance while you are doing the exercises, and how to take care of yourself when you have completed an exercise. Work carefully through this section and spend some time ensuring you know how to keep yourself safe before you begin the exercises in the rest of this book.

Before You Start the Exercises

Where to Begin

- We recommend that you do the exercises in the order they appear in the book. The chapters build on each other and follow the sequence we have found to be most helpful for survivors of sexual abuse. Sometimes you may want to go back and do some of the exercises again or occasionally you may need to jump ahead, for example to look at how to deal with a disturbing symptom such as a flashback.

- Some exercises may seem too frightening or too difficult. Don't force yourself to do exercises you don't feel ready for. You may be able to return to them later when you feel stronger or have more support. Not every exercise may be suitable or necessary for everyone to complete.
- The exercises in chapters 3 and 4 are intended to help you to understand more about the kind of difficult experiences and reactions survivors commonly have. Working through these chapters before moving on to the rest of the book will help you keep safe and feel more in control of what is happening to you.
- Many of the exercises are followed by examples and comments from other survivors. You might want to look through these before you begin an exercise.
- You can photocopy the exercises in this book. If you have more than one abuser you will need to repeat some of the exercises for each of your abusers.
- Refer back to this chapter before, during or after each exercise if you need to remind yourself of ways to keep safe and take care of yourself.

Getting Support

It may be hard to cope alone sometimes while you are working through this book. If you feel depressed, you may feel very alone and think that no one understands or wants to help. Often people are around—friends, family, local services and organizations—who would be willing to help. When you are feeling really bad it can be difficult to find out about services or to ask for help for the first time, so try to do this preparation work now. The Resources section lists some organizations that can provide help. National organizations often can give information about local affiliates. You could also ask your community health center or social services department about which resources are available in your area.

Getting help and support from others is a useful and practical way of dealing with your problems, not a sign of weakness and failure. You might want to ask a friend to act as a support person while you work through this book. If you do start to feel overwhelmed and cannot cope, seek professional help—your doctor will be able to advise you.

EXERCISE 1.1 SOURCES OF HELP

Purpose   To find sources of help for yourself and to have a ready-made list of contacts to refer to when you are feeling bad.

Make a list of people you could telephone when you are feeling bad. You may want to include national and local hotlines, friends, family members and professional workers who may be involved with your care. Your doctor should be contacted in case of emergency or if you are feeling suicidal; add his or her number to your list.

Name	Telephone number	Available when?

Also make a list of people or organizations you could visit or ask to visit you.

Name	Address/telephone number	Available when?

I think you have to be ready in your own mind for anything the exercises bring up and ask for help if you need it. —Lesley

Making Preparations

You will need to take time to do these exercises and prepare yourself for any strong emotional reactions. Set aside time to work through this book and do the exercises in a place where you feel safe and comfortable. For some of you, this may be somewhere where you are alone and undisturbed; others may want people around. Consider how much time you will devote to these exercises at one sitting. Give yourself plenty of time to work on the exercise and to deal with your reactions afterward. Do not expect to do too much at one time. These exercises can bring up powerful feelings and be very tiring. You may want a support person to be with you when you do the exercises or available afterward. Some survivors find comfort by having a special object, such as a plush toy, with them while they do the exercises. Think about what would feel best for you and make some notes below.

Place

_____

Time of day

_____

How much time to spend at one sitting?

_____

Who would you like with you?

_____

Who would you like to be available afterward?

_____

What special object would you like with you?

_____

I was reluctant to start the exercises. I was tense and panicky and aware that my husband was around. I overcame my difficulties in starting by asking my husband to go out (and I told him why). Then I could concentrate on the exercise.   —Maya

I did not want to do the exercises when I was alone or late at night.
—Rebecca

During the Exercises

This book is intended to help you understand and process your memories and feelings. This is not easy to do if you become flooded by your memories and overwhelmed by your feelings. Therefore, set a pace that is comfortable for you and approach the exercises from a safe emotional distance.

Going at Your Own Pace

There is no right speed at which you should progress through this workbook. Some people will work through the book quickly; others will complete the exercises slowly, maybe leaving gaps of time before moving on to the next section. It is up to you to set the pace that feels comfortable for you.

When should I slow down?   We suggest you slow down if you find yourself being overwhelmed by feelings, behaving in harmful ways or unable to process your thoughts and feelings. You may want to take a break from the exercises for a while. Some survivors return to the same exercises again and again before they feel ready to move on. If you begin to experience strong emotional or physical reactions, allow yourself time and space to understand and process these reactions before continuing with the next exercises.

When should I speed up?   It's important to work at your own pace rather than push yourself to work faster because you think you should. If you know other people who are using this workbook, try not to compare yourself with them. Everyone is unique in their reactions and needs. However, if you are picking up this workbook, doing a little and then forgetting about it for weeks and months, it may be helpful to look at why you might be avoiding doing this work and what reasons you are giving yourself for this. Look back at Exercise 1 on page 4.

> It helped me contain my feelings by working through the exercises in bursts, although I was always tempted to move on immediately to the next chapter. I also made sure I was in a safe place where I could contact people if I needed to.   —Thomas

> I found some of the exercises too powerful to do in one session, so I spaced them out over a couple of hours with some fun things in between.   —Rebecca

Finding a Safe Distance

> Learn how to feel safe before attempting the exercises.   —Rebecca

To do the exercises in this book, you will need to think about your past and get in touch with your feelings. If you have pushed your memories and feelings away or if you detach and feel numb while you are doing the exercises, you may want to get closer to your experiences now in order to work on them. On the other hand, if you are overwhelmed constantly by memories and feelings, then you may not be able to do the thinking required by these exercises or process what is happening to you. In short, if you are either too close to or too far from your feelings and experiences, you may have difficulty benefiting from these exercises. Below are a number of methods you can use to create the emotional distance that feels safe for you while doing these exercises.

Creating Distance from Your Experiences

Feeling overwhelmed by your feelings is distressing and can make it hard to do the exercises. It is helpful therefore to know how to distance yourself from your memories and feelings while you do these exercises. Pushing away your experiences and distracting yourself in the short term can be useful ways of protecting yourself and giving yourself a break from feeling bad. As you feel stronger, you may be able to repeat the exercises from a closer emotional position. Below is a list of ways to help you contain painful feelings, create distance and do the exercises in an emotionally cooler way.

You can cope with overwhelming memories and feelings by

- Trying to become aware of how you usually push your thoughts and feelings away or distract yourself, and then using these techniques consciously.
- Stopping in the middle of an exercise if necessary and using a coping strategy (see chapter 3).

Survivors have suggested the following techniques may be helpful to rid yourself of bad feelings symbolically and to contain painful memories for a while.

- Put your bad feelings on a rug or blanket and shake it outside.
- Run water over your wrists to wash away your feelings.
- Put your memories in a box and lock it.

Below are distancing techniques that can be used with exercises that ask you to write about yourself, think about an incident or person, or look at photographs.

- Imagine you are writing about someone else rather than yourself. Write in the third person; for example, "Mandy (rather than "I") has problems with eating; she binge-eats often when she is upset."
- Choose an incident that is not too distressing for you or that causes a level of distress you can cope with. You don't have to dive into the worst incidents first.
- If you have several abusers, work on the abuser you feel least frightened of or disturbed by first.
- If it feels too painful to think about yourself as a child, think about another child (a child you know or an imaginary child) rather than yourself.
- Look at incidents or people as though through the wrong end of a telescope or binoculars, so they appear smaller and farther away and have a less powerful effect on your emotions.
- Imagine you are watching the person (it may be you) or incident on a video and you have the remote control. You can stop or pause the video so you are in control of how much you see and hear.

> Use your own way of pushing away your memories or feelings to a safe distance. Keep going! Even if you are frightened like I was during the exercises, it does get better. It's worth it in the end. Repeat positive affirmations to yourself such as "I can do this and I will."
> —Maya

> When I feel really bad, I breathe in deeply, then blow my breath out through pursed lips. I try to blow all my bad feelings out into the air with my breath. Sometimes I wave my arms around myself to help push the bad feelings away.   —Alma

Getting Closer to the Experience

Use the techniques below only if you think you are too detached from your feelings or out of touch with your experiences.

- Look at photographs of yourself as a child, your abuser, your family or where you used to live.
- Spend time sitting quietly and try to become aware of what you are feeling.
- Focus on any body symptoms, such as tense shoulders; stay with the feeling and become aware of what is happening within you.
- Think about a specific incident or person from your past that relates to the exercise and again become aware of what you are feeling.
- Hold or look at a toy or a possession you had as a child.

Remember that pushing things away can also be a way of protecting yourself from overwhelming feelings, so stay in control and move only as close as you want to.

Taking Care of Yourself after Each Exercise

Take some time to look after yourself after each exercise. You may need to rest, talk to someone, get some support or find some other way of coping and taking care of yourself. Chapter 3 helps you develop nonharmful coping strategies. If you can't finish an exercise or don't feel like you've moved on after doing it, don't worry—you can try it again another time. It is normal to think a particular exercise hasn't changed anything for you. We can only change or see something in a new way when the time is right. Below, Maya shares her experiences of coping with the aftereffects of doing the exercises in this book:

- The exercise made me feel angry and I threw down the paper. I felt afraid and panicky. I played relaxing music to help me calm down. The fear increased at first—I shook all over. It took time for me to realize that nothing terrible would happen. Now I am proud of myself for doing it, and I feel stronger.
- After the exercise, I felt sad that no one had been around for me as a child, so I took care of myself by climbing into my sleeping bag with my favorite pillow and playing relaxing music.
- I was extremely frightened and thought I would be found out and punished for "lying" about the abuse. I talked to my counselor about my fears, and she supported me.
- Reward yourself after each exercise—you have taken a step toward self-understanding and personal growth. Good job!   —*Maya*

The exercise below is about creating an imaginary safe place where you can go whenever you need to. You could go to this safe place after you have completed an exercise, or whenever you feel frightened or overwhelmed.

EXERCISE 1.2 SAFE PLACE

Purpose   To create a safe place in your imagination that you can go to when you feel overwhelmed or unable to cope.

1) Choose a time when you are feeling reasonably OK and make yourself comfortable by lying down or sitting in a relaxed position.

2) Close your eyes and think about a place where you could be alone and feel safe, peaceful and relaxed. This could be a place that you know or a place that you imagine. Many people choose a place outdoors, such as a deserted beach or somewhere in the country. If you do not feel safe being on your own, imagine that a person you feel safe with is there also.

3) Imagine that you are lying down or sitting in this place and that you are feeling warm, relaxed and safe. Concentrate on all the sensations you are experiencing. What can you see (trees, the sky, the sea)? What can you hear (waves, birds)? What can you smell (flowers, the sea)? What can you feel (grass or sand beneath you)? Stay here for a while, absorbing all the sensations around you and enjoying the feeling of safety and relaxation. Remind yourself that you can come back to this place whenever you want to.

4) When you are ready, open your eyes and bring yourself back to where you really are by looking around the room. Now write down a description of your safe place below, and remember to include a description of what you could see, hear, smell and feel. You may want to draw or paint your safe place instead.

5) Practice going to this safe place at times when you are feeling OK until you are able to do this easily.

6) When you are feeling stressed, frightened or overwhelmed and you need a "time out," bring the image of your safe place to mind. You can do this wherever you are; you do not need to be in a special place, nor do you need to be lying down or sitting down.

My Safe Place

Examples of safe places

The air is fresh and clean, the sky clear blue. The sun shines through the trees, bringing light and warmth to my garden. A stream of clear water ripples over the stones. I love to sit by the stream and listen to the sound of the water—it sings a peaceful song as it travels along. I put my cares into the stream and they are carried away. The sweet perfume of the flower garden pervades the air, reminding me of the joy of being alive. It is a special garden where the wild animals roam around freely, keeping me safe from harm. The animals are my friends, they take care of me. They know when I am feeling weak—they know I will be at the stream. Gently and powerfully the lion and tiger come and rest beside me. I reach out and touch their soft fur. As I stroke them, I sense their protectiveness toward me—I am safe. The water carries away my burdens and I feel free. The lion and tiger remind me that I have strength within and that I am protected. I become re-energized. As I feel the warmth of the sun on my body, I feel myself becoming alive again.   —*Calli*

The place I imagined was on an island. It had ocean all around it. There was only one way in and that was by boat and I would see that. It had trees around with fruit on them. I had a house that I had built. I could hear birds singing. I was protected. Every so often, I would get all my friends to come and have a party. This is a nice, safe place.   —*Lesley*

My safe place is just after midnight on the beach with my wife. All the colored lights are still lit, but not a lot of people are around. I sit on the sand, which is still warm from the day's sun. There is the sound of seagulls flying around and the purring of the beach-cleaning vehicle to clean the sand for the next horde of vacation-seekers. Fishermen can be heard preparing their boats for the early morning trawl. A light breeze blowing every few seconds brings the smell of the cool, calm sea rippling toward us. I walk barefoot along the wet sand, leaving footprints in it as the tide slowly starts to come in. Turning around, I look back at the row of different amusement arcades lit up with hundreds of colored bulbs. No one else is around and the whole beach is ours. The sky is black with the twinkle of stars scattered around the banana-shaped moon. Slowly the night begins to cool and the breeze brings raised goosebumps on our arms. This tells me we are OK.   —*Graham*

I enjoyed going to my imaginary place and thinking about it. I've never done that before.   —*Lesley*

It's important to find a way to feel safe. I find it really hard to relax, and I never feel safe. I always watch my back and feel paranoid. My husband has started to help me get through this so that I can relax a little. My husband puts his arms around me and talks to me for a little while to reassure me that I am safe. Then I feel safe and relaxed. We are still working on this until I feel completely safe on my own.   —*Paula*

In this chapter, we have looked at ways of keeping safe and feeling more in control while working through this book. This is your journey and it will be challenging, but remember that whatever your feelings and reactions to the exercises, you are not alone. Learning to take care of your own needs and asking for help when necessary is an important part of the healing process. We wish you well.

How the Abuse Has Affected My Life

When children are being sexually abused, they experience many confusing and distressing feelings that can also affect the way they behave. As adults, many survivors continue to have problems as a result of their childhood abuse. The problems can affect every part of their lives: how they feel, the way they think, how they relate to other people and the things they do. They may feel helpless and overwhelmed by the chaos in their lives and think it is not possible to feel better about themselves or create a better life. Many survivors believe they have problems because they are stupid, crazy, difficult, mentally ill, unsociable, bad or because they were "born evil." Other people may have told them these things.

You may believe you have difficulties in your life because something is wrong with you instead of understanding that your current problems may be a result of your past experiences. In this chapter, we want to help you think more clearly about the problems you have had as an adult and understand how they might relate to your childhood abuse. Your problems are shared by many other survivors, and in this book, step by step, we hope you will learn how to begin to overcome your problems and look forward to a brighter future.

Effects of Childhood Abuse

The first exercise lists the problems that are most commonly reported by survivors of sexual abuse. However, it does not mean you have been sexually abused if you have any of these problems. This list cannot be used to "diagnose" sexual abuse.

EXERCISE 2.1 EFFECTS OF SEXUAL ABUSE

Purpose   To look at the ways that sexual abuse has affected your life and help you see that you share many of your problems with other survivors of childhood sexual abuse.

Below is a list of the problems that survivors most commonly report. Look through the list and for each problem indicate whether you currently experience this problem or if you experienced it in the past. At the end of the list add any other problems that you experience.

Problems	Applies to you?			
	Yes	A little	No	Not now
Fears				
Anxiety				
Phobias				
Nervousness				
Nightmares				
Sleep problems				
Depression				
Shame				
Guilt				
Feeling like a victim				
Lack of self-confidence				
Feeling different from others				
Feeling self-conscious				
Feeling unable to take action or change situations				
Feeling dirty				
Obsessed with cleaning or washing				
Constant anxious thoughts				
Suicide attempts				
Self-harming (such as slashing arms)				
Blackouts				
Fits, seizures				
Gaps in everyday memory				

Problems	Applies to you?			
	Yes	A little	No	Not now
Binge-eating	_____	_____	_____	_____
Self-induced vomiting	_____	_____	_____	_____
Compulsive eating	_____	_____	_____	_____
Anorexia nervosa	_____	_____	_____	_____
Obsessed with body image	_____	_____	_____	_____
No interest in sex	_____	_____	_____	_____
Fear of sex	_____	_____	_____	_____
Avoiding specific sexual activities	_____	_____	_____	_____
Feeling unable to say "No" to sex	_____	_____	_____	_____
Obsessed with sex	_____	_____	_____	_____
Aggressive sexual behavior	_____	_____	_____	_____
Flashbacks (feeling of reliving parts of the past)	_____	_____	_____	_____
Hearing the abuser's voice when he or she isn't there	_____	_____	_____	_____
Seeing the abuser's face when he or she isn't there	_____	_____	_____	_____
Confusion about sexual orientation (homosexual or heterosexual)	_____	_____	_____	_____
Confusion about sexual identity (male or female)	_____	_____	_____	_____
Unable to get close to people	_____	_____	_____	_____
Marrying young to get away from home	_____	_____	_____	_____
Relationship problems	_____	_____	_____	_____
Excessive concerns about security of home or self	_____	_____	_____	_____
Alcohol problems	_____	_____	_____	_____
Drug problems	_____	_____	_____	_____
Employment problems	_____	_____	_____	_____

(continued)

Problems	Applies to you?			
	Yes	A little	No	Not now
Being re-victimized	_____	_____	_____	_____
Criminal involvement	_____	_____	_____	_____
Needing to be in control	_____	_____	_____	_____
Delinquency	_____	_____	_____	_____
Aggressive behavior	_____	_____	_____	_____
Bullying	_____	_____	_____	_____
Abusing others	_____	_____	_____	_____
Clinging and being extremely dependent	_____	_____	_____	_____
Anger	_____	_____	_____	_____
Hostility	_____	_____	_____	_____
Problems communicating	_____	_____	_____	_____
Working too hard	_____	_____	_____	_____
Distrusting people	_____	_____	_____	_____
Difficulty in being able to judge people's trustworthiness	_____	_____	_____	_____
Difficulties relating to children	_____	_____	_____	_____
Other problems	_____	_____	_____	_____

Remember these are the ways you survived your abuse. Try not to be upset by all the "Yes" responses—you can work on the underlying problems one at a time.   —Calli

You may have checked just a few of the problems on the list, or many. You may be pleased to realize you have overcome some of the difficulties you experienced in the past. It is normal to have problems as a result of traumatic experiences or inappropriate and abusive relationships. Seeing that you share your problems with other survivors can help you realize that your problems may be a result of your abusive experiences rather than because something is wrong with you. Being abused and unprotected as a child often results in adult survivors having difficulties in their relationships with children; this issue is explored further in chapter 10.

Many of the problems on the list above relate to things that you *do* (such as self-harming, avoiding sex, drinking too much); however, another important consequence of sexual abuse is the impact it has on the way you *feel*. The next two exercises explore the effects of sexual abuse on your feelings about yourself and your relationship to your emotions.

Feelings about Yourself

Survivors often feel worthless because of how they were treated by their abusers and sometimes because of the lack of support or protection from other adults. The way survivors think about the abuse also affects the way they feel about themselves. Many survivors believe they are responsible for the abuse and this leaves them feeling guilty and ashamed. In the next exercise you are asked to think about how you feel about yourself now.

EXERCISE 2.2 FEELINGS ABOUT YOURSELF

Purpose   To help you become more aware of how you feel about yourself.
Look through the following list of statements and circle the number that corresponds to how much you agree with each one. For example:

- If you totally agree, circle 0.
- If you neither agree nor disagree, circle 5.
- If you totally disagree, circle 10.

Feelings about myself	*Agree*					*?*			*Disagree*		
I hate myself	0	1	2	3	4	5	6	7	8	9	10
I don't like myself	0	1	2	3	4	5	6	7	8	9	10
I feel worthless	0	1	2	3	4	5	6	7	8	9	10
I don't accept myself	0	1	2	3	4	5	6	7	8	9	10
I am bad	0	1	2	3	4	5	6	7	8	9	10
I do not like the child I was	0	1	2	3	4	5	6	7	8	9	10
I do not feel positive about the future	0	1	2	3	4	5	6	7	8	9	10
I feel helpless	0	1	2	3	4	5	6	7	8	9	10

Your Relationship to Your Feelings

The powerful emotions a child experiences during sexual abuse can also
have long-term effects on survivors' lives. As adults, survivors may still
experience emotions such as anxiety, guilt, anger, helplessness, confusion,
terror or depression. They often find it difficult to deal with these
powerful feelings and may feel very uncomfortable with them. Some
survivors feel overwhelmed and frightened by their feelings while others
cope by detaching from their feelings; they only feel "numb." The next
exercise helps you explore your relationship with your feelings. In the last
chapter of this workbook, you will be asked to rate your feelings again to
assess any changes.

EXERCISE 2.3 YOUR RELATIONSHIP TO YOUR FEELINGS

Purpose   To help you focus on the way you relate to your feelings.
    Look through the following list of statements and circle the number
that corresponds to how much you agree with each one. For example,

- If you totally agree, circle 0.
- If you neither agree nor disagree, circle 5.
- If you totally disagree, circle 10.

My Feelings	Agree					?			Disagree		
I am overwhelmed by my feelings	0	1	2	3	4	5	6	7	8	9	10
I am not in touch with my feelings	0	1	2	3	4	5	6	7	8	9	10
I am frightened of my own feelings	0	1	2	3	4	5	6	7	8	9	10
I am cut off from my feelings	0	1	2	3	4	5	6	7	8	9	10
I am ill at ease with my feelings	0	1	2	3	4	5	6	7	8	9	10

At this stage, we are simply trying to help you understand what
problems you have and why you have them. The exercises in the rest of

this book are designed to help you work through your feelings, take control of your symptoms and tackle the causes of the problems.

Survivors are affected by abuse in different ways. As individuals with different experiences, each person will have found his or her own way of surviving the abuse. The severity of a survivor's problems also relates to the circumstances of the abuse, such as the age of the child, the relationship with the abuser, the number of abusers, the type of abuse and the resources available to the child. A child from a caring family abused by a stranger is in a different situation and has access to more resources than a child abused by both parents with no caring adult available to him or her. Each child will be affected differently and will find his or her own way of coping.

How Does Sexual Abuse Cause These Problems?

Researcher and author David Finkelhor has tried to explain how sexual abuse affects children and leads to the long-term problems we discussed earlier. Finkelhor suggests four processes in childhood sexual abuse that cause problems: Traumatic sexualization, stigmatization, betrayal and powerlessness (Finkelhor, 1986). This model helps explain how sexual abuse can fundamentally affect a person's life, and we discuss it in more detail in our book *Surviving Childhood Sexual Abuse*.

EXERCISE 2.4 FINKELHOR'S FOUR PROCESSES

Purpose   To help you understand how problems develop in survivors' lives.

This exercise uses Finkelhor's model to help you see how sexual abuse is a traumatic experience that leads to the development of many problems in survivors' lives. Finkelhor's four processes are described briefly below. After each one, you are asked to think about your own problems and feelings and write down which of your problems may have resulted from each process.

Traumatic Sexualization

When children are sexually abused, they are exposed to sexual experiences that are inappropriate or too advanced for their age or development level. Their sexual experience, knowledge and identity are not allowed to develop naturally. They are given confusing and incorrect messages about sexual behavior. Their early experiences of sexual behavior and sexuality may be traumatic. The physical and emotional pain involved in sexual abuse for many children means that sex becomes associated with bad feelings. Sometimes, however, children enjoy parts of the touching and many experience sexual pleasure and orgasm.

As a result of their inappropriate sexual experiences, survivors can grow up confused about their own sexual feelings and normal sexual behavior. This leads to sexual difficulties in adults, ranging from fears and phobias about sex to preoccupation and obsessions with sex.

Write down any of your problems that result from traumatic sexualization:

_____

_____

_____

_____

_____

_____

_____

_____

_____

_____

Examples

When I was at school, I thought everyone knew I was getting abused. I used to sleep with anybody because the abuse made me think that was how I had to be around boys and men. I live with a man and have two children but I have had relationships with three women. I am very confused about my sexuality.   —Lesley

I am ashamed of my own body. I never liked undressing in front of anyone. At school I would be punished because I refused to change for gym or take a shower. I am unable to relax and enjoy sex with my wife. I have no interest in sex at all.   —Graham

It is difficult to work on sexual difficulties until you have worked on the problems resulting from the other three processes described below. Sexual difficulties are not specifically covered in this book but are discussed in our book *Surviving Childhood Sexual Abuse.*

Stigmatization

Some children who are sexually abused may believe for a while that what is happening to them is "normal." However, most child victims feel the abuse is wrong and shameful at some point, even when they don't understand exactly what is happening. Abusers may blame children for the abuse, tell them to keep the abuse secret and frighten them into silence. This secrecy makes children feel that there is something to feel guilty and ashamed about. Other people who are told or find out about the abuse may be shocked and blame the victim or put pressure on him or her to remain silent. This can add to the feeling of shame. Adult survivors often continue to keep the secret for fear of other people's reactions and because they feel ashamed.

As a result of the stigmatization process, many survivors blame themselves for the abuse. They may also feel responsible and guilty for anything bad that happens to them or to other people they know. Survivors have told us they feel "dirty" and ashamed because of the things that have been done to them. Survivors often feel bad about themselves and different from other people. They may therefore isolate themselves from other people and avoid making close friendships. The feelings of shame and guilt can lead survivors to abuse and punish themselves with drugs, alcohol or through self-mutilation and suicide attempts. Some survivors feel so different that they see themselves as outsiders in society, unable to care about what happens to them or what they do. Survivors who feel like this may start to behave in criminal or antisocial ways and end up in court or prison.

Write down any problems you have that result from stigmatization:

_____

_____

_____

_____

_____

_____

_____

_____

_____

Examples

> I used to get involved in dangerous games like playing with fire, jumping out of windows in high buildings and hitchhiking. I'd numbed myself from my abuse, had no sense of danger and didn't care about my safety. My abusers didn't respect or care about me, so I didn't believe I was important either. —*Sarah*

> The abuse has made me very critical of myself and I cannot accept myself. It is difficult for me to accept a pat on the back. I feel people are just being nice to me, not that I've done something to deserve praise. —*Anita B.*

> I have had drinking and drug problems—it's a nice feeling to forget for a while. —*Lesley*

> I feel ashamed and unclean. I have a problem with cleanliness; I brush my teeth about eight times a day and I never feel satisfied that the house is clean enough. —*Graham*

Chapters 5 to 7 are designed to help you work on the feelings of guilt and shame resulting from stigmatization.

Betrayal

When children are abused, especially by relatives or someone they know or like, their trust is betrayed. Abusers often build up trusting relationships with children and may make them feel wanted and cared for before abusing them. They manipulate the trust and vulnerability of children and disregard their well-being. Child and adult survivors may also feel betrayed by nonabusing mothers, family, friends and professionals who do not support and protect them.

Betrayal can be experienced as a feeling of loss—loss of a trusting and loving relationship—and this can lead to feelings of grief and depression, or anger and hostility. Fear of betrayal can also lead to mistrust of others and cause survivors to withdraw or feel uncomfortable in close relationships. On the other hand, some survivors become extremely dependent and clingy.

Being betrayed by the very people one would expect to be able to trust can result in survivors having difficulties in trusting other people. They may not be able to trust or they may have difficulties knowing who can be trusted. This in turn makes the survivors vulnerable to further abuse and exploitation, especially if they are unable to judge trustworthiness or feel compelled to cling to bad relationships.

Write down any of your problems that result from betrayal:

_____

_____

_____

_____

_____

_____

_____

_____

_____

_____

Examples

> It is hard for me to have friendships. It is hard for me to trust people. I always think they are lying to me. It's hard for me to show my children love, but you cannot show love if you have never been shown it. I'm learning how to do this.   —*Lesley*

> I feel angry toward people and I don't trust many people. I am overprotective about my children and won't let them stay overnight at a friend's house.   —*Paula*

Chapters 8 and 9 help you begin to work on issues of betrayal by exploring your relationships with your abusers and with your mother or other nonabusing caregivers.

Powerlessness

Children experience an intense sense of powerlessness during sexual abuse. Children's bodies are touched or invaded and this may happen again and again. Abusers manipulate children and may physically force them into abuse. Children feel powerless to stop the abuse or reveal what is happening. Even when children do tell, they may not be believed. Children repeatedly experience fear and an inability to control the situation.

The powerlessness experienced in sexual abuse can lead to long-term feelings of being unable to take action or change situations. Survivors thus feel powerless to prevent further abuse and may end up feeling like victims all their lives. Feeling powerless and out of control can produce panic attacks, anxiety, phobias and nightmares. Survivors may try to escape from their fears and feelings of powerlessness by running away from home or from school, or by withdrawing emotionally. Emotional withdrawal can take the form of depression, blanking out or blacking out, or living in a fantasy world.

Survivors may also react to feeling powerless by attempting to take control and by making themselves feel more powerful in some way. Eating disorders often involve a desperate attempt to exert some control, by controlling one's food intake and body weight. Obsessive-compulsive behaviors, such as excessive counting, checking or cleaning, can also be ways of coping with feeling out of control. Some survivors try to feel more powerful by aggressive behavior, by bullying, being abusive or by controlling other people.

Write down any of your problems that result from powerlessness:

_____

_____

_____

_____

_____

_____

_____

_____

_____

_____

Examples

The problems I have that result from feeling powerless are flashbacks, phobias, anxiety, feeling like a victim, obsessed with cleaning, needing to be in control.   —*Paula*

I feel weak and unimportant, and it's hard for me to make decisions. I experience flashbacks, hallucinations, bad dreams and panic attacks. —*Graham*

Chapter 7 helps you see that you have more power now than you did when you were a child. The exercises in chapter 8 are intended to help you feel more empowered in relation to your abuser.

It was hard for me to control my feelings when I was doing this
exercise. I had flashbacks—my mind wandered off to what happened.
I was scared and angry and wanted revenge on my abusers. I calmed
myself down by telling myself I am in control now. It also helped to
have someone in the room with me who understood what I have
been through. Also I went back to chapter 1 and looked at the ways I
could take care of myself. —*Paula*

Childhood abuse is a traumatic event that has many different effects on
the lives of survivors. Some of the effects are a direct result of the abuse,
such as feeling guilty, having flashbacks or hallucinations, being confused
about sexual orientation or identity, being overprotective of children,
feeling depressed or having problems trusting other people. Other
problems arise indirectly as a result of the ways survivors cope with the
abuse. When people feel bad or have bad experiences, they have to find
some way of coping with them. Survivors often cope with their memories
and feelings about the abuse by drinking alcohol, keeping busy, working
hard, cutting themselves, eating a lot or pushing their memories away.
Nearly all of these coping strategies start off as useful ways of coping
with bad experiences, but some can develop into problems in their
own right.

Many survivors see their current problems as signs that something is
wrong with them or that they are bad people, rather than understanding
that the problems may be a result of the abuse or of the creative ways they
have used to cope with and survive the abuse. The next exercise asks you
to think about your past and current problems and to relate them to your
past experiences. This is to help you understand that your symptoms were
a response to how you were feeling and what was happening to you at
different times in your life.

EXERCISE 2.5 HOW THE ABUSE
HAS AFFECTED MY LIFE

Purpose   To help you look at past and current problems and to relate
them to your abusive experiences.

1) Think about yourself at different ages, from childhood to the
   present. Remember what was happening to you at these times
   and try to relate your symptoms and problems to your experiences. Remember that some of the problems will have resulted
   from the way you were treated (for example, feeling bad about

yourself or flashbacks) and others will be ways you tried to survive and cope with your feelings (for example, self-harm or working too hard).

2) Write about the kinds of difficulties you have experienced and how you think they relate to the abuse.

The example that follows may help you. Some of you may prefer to draw a diagram or use one of the other alternatives to writing.

How the abuse has affected my life:

_____

_____

_____

_____

_____

_____

_____

_____

_____

_____

Catherine's example

I always felt different from other children, but I didn't know why at the time. The abuse had made me feel unworthy, which made it hard for me to make friends. I felt aggressive toward younger children and any friends I did manage to make. If I hadn't been abused, I wouldn't have grown up feeling different from other children and I wouldn't have felt like no one liked me or wanted to be my friend. I had a poor self-image.

Later on, in adolescence, my low self-esteem made me feel ugly, and I used to worry that no boy would ever be interested in me. Because of what the abuse taught me, I let boys use my body without respect for me. When I was fifteen, I remember having a bag of broken glass, hidden under my bed, ready. I slashed my arms to get rid of the emotional pain I couldn't understand. I also remember drinking bottles of wine on my own at that age.

Life at college was a nightmare. Being away from the abusive situation was opportunity for my emotions to surface. I was very mixed up and I developed anorexia nervosa, then bulimia nervosa. I was socially inept. I lived on my own in a rented room and I had no friends. It was three years of hell. I buried myself in my work—it was all I knew how to do.

Later on I had relationship problems. Guys could do what they liked with me—why not? It was what I had learned from the abuser—I was there for others, not for me. I had difficulties in my marriage. I was emotionally demanding, clingy and very dependent. I could not return the physical love my husband offered; I thought this was something he did to me and I was conditioned into blanking out whenever things got intimate. The slashing and other self-injury started again. If I hadn't been abused, I wouldn't have suffered the bouts of depression, the feelings of despair and nothingness, time after time. There was some new problem every six months or so. Always something around the corner to stop any growth in my self-esteem and confidence.

Looking toward the Future

This is how Rebecca described her problems at the beginning of therapy:

> The abuse really affected my life. My childhood was lost and now I experience depression, anger, frustration and constant fear. I feel I am totally worthless, useless and have no right to live. It has destroyed my ability to love and care and left me with a compulsive need to be in control of everything and everyone. I feel afraid I will abuse other people to gain that control. I hate myself, my body and my spirit because I am evil and rotten through and through. I don't think I will ever be able to experience a full relationship with someone and that makes me angry. I want to hurt myself all the time.

Rebecca now writes:

> The writing above was how I felt when I came into therapy. Some of the problems were not due to the sexual abuse but to other experiences in my childhood. It makes me very sad to see how I was so obviously very deeply depressed and could not see any hope at all. Now I realize just how far I have come. The changes have not always been easy to see. I don't self-injure anymore. The depression I have lived with all my life has begun to take a back seat. I don't wish I were dead anymore. That has to be good. Today I feel good in general. I am

now very close to discontinuing my antidepressant medication, which I have taken for the last five years. My mood swings are less severe and much less frequent. I have learned to talk about how I am feeling, which is the most positive improvement. I have also learned to laugh and cry—emotions I found difficult to express before.

I don't blame myself for the abuse I suffered any more, and I don't immediately blame myself if things go wrong. It is getting easier to have relationships and I am moving toward those relationships (sexual) that for me are most full of difficulty. My friendships are more equal and productive. I generally feel good about myself and my body. This is not true every day, but who feels good all the time? My life is very different now, I have a job (a good professional position) and I am able to make plans for my future career. I am even planning to start a graduate program in the next year. Today the world looks very different. I am more optimistic about my future and I have achieved what I set out to do—feel content and satisfied with who I am.

You have looked back at what has happened to you in the past and seen the range of problems resulting from your experiences. It may be that some of your problems are related to experiences in your life besides the sexual abuse. It is hard to know which problems are caused by the abuse and impossible to know what you would be like now if you hadn't been abused. What is possible, though, is to work on your current problems and to take some control of the way your life goes from now on. You are already moving toward this by working through this book.

Becoming aware of the extent of your problems can be very distressing. The problems you have may be a result of the abuse or how you learned to cope with your painful experiences. Remind yourself that it is normal to have problems when you have experienced abuse or trauma and, like Rebecca, you can begin to overcome them. The next chapter helps you understand more about the coping strategies you use and also helps you to begin to replace harmful coping strategies with less harmful ones.

Before you move on, notice how you are feeling now and take care of yourself.

Coping Strategies 3

Everyone who faces problems, bad experiences and painful feelings has to find ways to cope with them. We might confide in another person, try to solve the problem, seek help and advice, or comfort and take care of ourselves. Children who are sexually abused usually cannot speak up or stop what is happening, however; they may have nowhere to go for comfort and support. To cope, these children often try to block thoughts and feelings about the abuse as a way of controlling their emotional pain. Blocking can be a necessary survival strategy in situations from which there is no escape. For many survivors, unfortunately, blocking becomes a habit they carry into adult life. It can create problems in the long term.

This chapter helps you understand more about the coping strategies that you use currently, consciously or unconsciously, to deal with painful memories and feelings about being sexually abused. Some of your strategies may be harming you, and we encourage you to look for less harmful ways of coping and to use your strategies with greater awareness.

First we look at the blocking strategies survivors commonly use. Then we consider expressing and processing strategies that are more helpful to use in the long term. The exercises in this chapter and the rest of the book are meant to help you express and process your thoughts and feelings rather than bury them.

Types of Coping Strategies

Blocking Strategies

People use all kinds of strategies to block out memories and feelings or to distract their attention. Abusing alcohol, drugs and food are common ways that people forget their problems and alter the way they feel. Keeping busy, going out all the time, cleaning, compulsively caring for others, sleeping or self-harming until the physical pain becomes greater than the emotional pain can serve the same purpose.

These ways of coping often become automatic responses to distressing feelings and problems. Survivors may not consciously understand why they do these things. Sometimes they start to believe that they must be "crazy" or "bad."

A major problem with coping strategies that block memories and feelings is, they never resolve the underlying difficulty. What's more, these coping strategies may develop into problems in their own right; for example, as an addiction or obsession. However, some blocking strategies can be useful if used in moderation and as a short-term measure; for example, to take a break from problems or to enable you to finish certain tasks, such as going to work.

Dissociation

Many survivors use the dissociation strategy as children and as adults to escape painful thoughts and feelings. They separate a part of themselves from what is happening and from their distress and pain. Some children describe stepping outside their bodies and watching themselves being abused without experiencing any of the physical and emotional pain. Others invent a fantasy world into which they can retreat every time they are being abused. Some survivors create different parts of themselves to hold different memories and feelings and to cope with different situations.

> The hurt started when I was about three years old, when my dad started to come into the bathroom to wash my hair. His excuse was that he had to check that I had washed myself "down there." I told my mom he was hurting me, but I did not tell her how he was hurting me. She insisted that he keep washing my hair. I had to forget the hurt, so I used to turn off and talk to a friend inside myself that I had created. Her name was "Baby" and she took most of the hurt.   —Jean

Dissociation is a way in which children cope with continuing abuse and in which adult survivors detach from their painful thoughts and memories about the abuse. Many survivors who dissociate are not aware of how much they are doing this.

Expressing and Processing Strategies

The exercises in this book ask you to take a different approach to dealing with your pain. They ask you to write, talk, paint or use other nonverbal ways of expressing yourself. Instead of blocking or distracting you from your feelings and memories, they help you to experience and express them—and to learn to think and feel in a new way about your past.

> The exercises helped me to get in touch with my feelings and break through my denial and minimization. They helped me release pent-up emotions in appropriate ways.   —Sarah

As a child, you were probably unable to express your thoughts and feelings about the abuse directly because you had to keep it a secret. This was not right, and as an adult you can choose to do something different. Writing, talking and painting are nonharmful coping strategies you can learn to use in your everyday life, not only when you are doing these exercises. Some people find it helps to keep a journal in which to note their feelings every day. Survivors have also recommended dancing, singing, sculpting and listening to music as ways of getting in touch with and releasing their feelings.

Self-Care and Support Strategies

With this workbook, we want to encourage you to understand more about what you want and need, to seek comfort and support from others and to learn to look after yourself. Some strategies, such as walking outside or having a massage, are ways of taking care of yourself, strengthening yourself physically and emotionally, and balancing the painful and difficult work you are doing with reminding yourself of the positive things in life. When you were sexually abused, your physical and emotional needs were ignored. You may have also learned ways to block your feelings and to numb the physical pain you felt. All these things can start a pattern of not caring for yourself and not attending to your own needs.

Coping strategies often become automatic reactions to feelings and hardships. You may not always be aware of what is happening or why you feel compelled to act in a certain way. Behaviors can serve different functions. They cannot always be put into one category, such as blocking or expressing and processing or self-care and support. Sleeping, for example, can be a way of blocking and also a way of taking care of yourself.

The exercises below are designed to help you become aware of the strategies you are currently using and why, and to strengthen your use of expressing and self-care strategies.

EXERCISE 3.1
IDENTIFYING YOUR COPING STRATEGIES

Purpose   To look at the different ways you deal with feelings, memories and problems.

The list below shows different ways that people cope with feelings, memories and problems. Look at the list. For each strategy, rate how frequently you use it by putting a checkmark under one of the columns. Add any other ways you cope with difficulties, and rate how often you use these strategies. Some of these strategies (for example, self-harm) could be problems in themselves, but for now record *all* the strategies you use, whether or not they are problematic.

Strategies	Applies to you?				
	Often	*Sometimes*	*Hardly ever*	*Never*	*Used to but don't now*
Cleaning (house or self)	_____	_____	_____	_____	_____
Sleeping	_____	_____	_____	_____	_____
Keeping busy	_____	_____	_____	_____	_____
Going out a lot	_____	_____	_____	_____	_____
Staying in a lot	_____	_____	_____	_____	_____
Sealing off feelings	_____	_____	_____	_____	_____
Fantasizing/ daydreaming	_____	_____	_____	_____	_____
Dissociating/ cutting off	_____	_____	_____	_____	_____
Passing out	_____	_____	_____	_____	_____
Taking medication	_____	_____	_____	_____	_____
Drinking alcohol	_____	_____	_____	_____	_____
Taking non-prescription drugs	_____	_____	_____	_____	_____
Smoking	_____	_____	_____	_____	_____

Strategies

Applies to you?

	Often	Sometimes	Hardly ever	Never	Used to but don't now
Self-harming	_____	_____	_____	_____	_____
Withdrawing from other people	_____	_____	_____	_____	_____
Overeating/ binge eating	_____	_____	_____	_____	_____
Undereating/ starving	_____	_____	_____	_____	_____
Working on computer	_____	_____	_____	_____	_____
Working	_____	_____	_____	_____	_____
Suicide attempts	_____	_____	_____	_____	_____
Becoming aggressive	_____	_____	_____	_____	_____
Having a bath	_____	_____	_____	_____	_____
Resting	_____	_____	_____	_____	_____
Painting how I feel	_____	_____	_____	_____	_____
Writing	_____	_____	_____	_____	_____
Phoning someone	_____	_____	_____	_____	_____
Talking to someone	_____	_____	_____	_____	_____
Walking	_____	_____	_____	_____	_____
Having a massage	_____	_____	_____	_____	_____
Exercising	_____	_____	_____	_____	_____
Dancing	_____	_____	_____	_____	_____
Listening to music	_____	_____	_____	_____	_____
Reading	_____	_____	_____	_____	_____

Survivors' comments

I realized how much I do when I am trying to cope with things.
—*Lesley*

It enabled me to look seriously at all the coping strategies I either engage in or had engaged in before. I was shocked to see how many I used. It is important to see things as they really are in order to get better.   —*Rebecca*

Benefits and Problems of Coping Strategies

We have seen that different strategies can be used to deal with feelings and difficulties. Some strategies—for example, keeping a journal—may be helpful and cause no additional problems. Other strategies, although helpful, can also have their problems or downsides; or they may be helpful if used in moderation but cause additional problems if they are used in excess.

I started to drink alcohol to block out my feelings about the abuse. I thought it would be an escape for me; however, it never was—it only made me worse. As a result, I got into trouble with the authorities; that is, the police, courts, the justice system and so on. My behavior led to probation orders and curfews and being barred from all bars. These restrictions only aggravated the way I was feeling, so I abused alcohol even more—drinking at home and finding other places where I could drink, like the next county, where the police didn't know me. I have also ended up in mental institutions over the years and been admitted to detox for six weeks, which helped a little but didn't stop me from drinking because I still had deep feelings about the abuse.
—*Anthony*

Anthony started to drink alcohol when he was fifteen. At first he had found drinking a moderate amount of alcohol was a useful coping strategy because it helped him block out his memories and feelings about being abused. Over time, however, Anthony developed a problem with alcohol itself—he became physically and psychologically dependent on it and got into trouble when he was drunk. Eventually Anthony had a number of other problems to cope with in addition to the abuse, and he began to see the downside of using alcohol as a coping strategy.

Anthony joined a childhood sexual abuse survivors' group. He began to understand more about his feelings and experiences and to develop less harmful ways of coping.

> I have not been in any real trouble since starting therapy. I no longer blame myself for being abused, and I do not bottle things up or keep them to myself anymore. I have more control over myself, and my life now in general is much better. —*Anthony*

Sarah, Paula and Lesley have also learned more about their ways of coping and can see how their strategies help but can also cause problems.

> I cope by blotting out my feelings. It helps at the time, but then my feelings catch up with me and I overreact. It also makes it hard to do anything about a situation when the impact doesn't hit you until later.
> —*Sarah*

> Eating chocolate calms my nerves, but in the long run I just want more chocolate to forget other things. —*Paula*

> Although keeping busy takes my mind off my feelings, sometimes I don't have time for my family. —*Lesley*

EXERCISE 3.2
BENEFITS AND PROBLEMS OF YOUR COPING STRATEGIES

Purpose   To understand how your coping strategies help you and how they might also cause problems.

Write down the coping strategies you use under the first column. Think about how each coping strategy helps and write this under the second column. Now think about what problems (if any) might result from this strategy. Record those thoughts under the third column. It might help you to look at Rebecca's example at the end of the exercise.

Coping strategy	How it helps	Downside/problems
Examples		
Drinking alcohol	Helps me forget the abuse. Makes me feel more confident	Doesn't solve the problem. Addiction, More problems when I'm drunk
Cutting self	Relieves tension. Changes emotional pain to physical pain	Scars I can't get rid of. Embarrassed when people see them

(continued)

Coping strategy	How it helps	Downside/problems
_____	_____	_____
_____	_____	_____
_____	_____	_____
_____	_____	_____
_____	_____	_____
_____	_____	_____
_____	_____	_____
_____	_____	_____
_____	_____	_____
_____	_____	_____
_____	_____	_____

Rebecca's example.   Rebecca's example is recorded in full so you can see the range of coping strategies one person might have. Her example continues to Exercise 3.3.

Coping strategy	How it helps	Downside/problems
Bathing	Relieves tension. Gives space to think in	None
Resting	Gives space to think	Can be just a way of escaping
Cleaning	Physical release of tension. Sense of achievement	Can become an obsession if taken too far. OK in moderation
Painting	Release of emotional pain and expression of feeling	None
Writing	Can make order out of confusion. Naming of feelings. Gives some focus for solution	None
Sleeping	Escape from emotional pain	Pain still has to be faced on waking

Coping strategy	How it helps	Downside/problems
Keeping busy	No time to dwell on problem	OK in moderation. Can become a way to avoid the problem or feelings
Staying in	Avoids other problems and people	Leads to further depression, bad feelings and difficulty communicating
Medication	Reduces physical and emotional pain	None in moderation. Can lead to psychological and physical dependency
Distraction	Takes mind off problem	None as long as problem is not ignored
Drinking alcohol	Reduces anxiety, dulls feelings	In excess leads to dependency, physical problems
Becoming aggressive	Reduces tension	Depression. Damage to others and to property
Withdrawing from others	Gives physical space to think	Cuts down possibility of looking at difficulty objectively and isolates
Overeating/bingeing	Quick way to suppress anxiety and bad feelings	Health and weight problems. Makes me feel unattractive. Low self-esteem
Undereating/starving	Greater feeling of self-control	Illness. False sense of control
Phone/talk to someone	Sharing problem. Gain support. Relieve feelings of anxiety	None, unless you expect others to solve the problem
Exercise	Relieves tension. Feeling of achievement	None in moderation
Working on computer	Relieves tension. Moves focus away from feeling or problem	None, as long as it's not used as a long-term escape
Sculpture	Achievement. Relieves anxiety. Focuses attention on expressing feelings	None

Survivors' comments

It took time to think about each strategy and how it made me feel. I don't think I have ever spent time on this level of analysis. It helped me see strategies that were helpful and unhelpful and how. I felt that I still use a lot of negative/unhelpful ways of coping. I was sad about this, but I accepted them. I could also identify a few good strategies that I had developed. —*Rebecca*

By doing this exercise, I realized that the things I do make some sense. —*Lesley*

It is important for all of us to have coping strategies to use during difficult times. Some coping strategies are harmless, some are harmless if used in moderation, and some coping strategies can be harmful and go on to become problems in their own right. It is obviously better to try to use coping strategies that will not cause you more harm. In the short term, however, you may have a hard time not using harmful coping strategies. Don't worry about it. For now, you are only trying to become more aware of ways in which your coping strategies help or cause problems.

EXERCISE 3.3 WHICH OF YOUR COPING STRATEGIES ARE HARMFUL?

Purpose To figure out which strategies are nonharmful and which strategies are generally harmful, or harmful if used in excess.

Refer to how you described each of your coping strategies in Exercise 3.2. Now sort them into the three categories below. Use your own judgment about whether the strategies are harmful. Different people will judge their own strategies differently.

Nonharmful

_____

_____

_____

_____

_____

Harmless in moderation but harmful in excess

_____

_____

_____

_____

_____

_____

Generally harmful or a problem

_____

_____

_____

_____

_____

_____

Examples

Rebecca

Nonharmful

Bathing	Phone someone
Painting	Talk to someone
Writing	Working on computer
Sculpture	

Harmless in moderation but harmful in excess

Exercising	Keeping busy
Distracting	Medication
Resting	Cleaning
Sleeping	

Generally harmful or a problem

Staying in	Overeating/bingeing
Drinking alcohol	Undereating/starving
Becoming aggressive	Withdrawal from others

(*continued*)

Wakefield Survivors' Moving On Group

Nonharmful

Bathing	Dancing
Resting	Listening to music
Writing	Phoning someone
Drawing	Talking to someone

Harmless in moderation but harmful in excess

Sleeping	Distracting
Taking medication	Withdrawing from other people
Exercising	Working hard
Keeping busy	Relentless joking around
Blotting out	Listening to other people's feelings/problems

Generally harmful or problematic

Self-harming	Exploding at others
Smoking	Pretending the abuse didn't happen

Survivors' comments

I found the exercise was helpful. It enabled me to categorize coping strategies and see where I stood. It was hard to decide which fitted into which category, but I assessed where they should go for me personally. I completed the exercise at a time when I was having to rely on these strategies to survive. I became very concerned when I realized that some of the things that I felt were helping at that moment were not, and that it was difficult to access the strategies that were nonharmful. —Rebecca

I know some things are harmful—like smoking or not eating, or taking too many pills—harmful for the body. But some things, like crying and talking, I feel are bad because I have been told not to do them. —Bronwyn

It made me realize how many positive ways there are to cope instead of negative ones. Be as honest as you can about how you cope and whether it is negative or positive. For example, starving is a negative way of coping, although sometimes if I am losing weight it seems positive and a good idea at the time. —Coral

I admitted to myself that I do some things that are harmful. —Lesley

EXERCISE 3.4 MY LIST OF
NONHARMFUL COPING STRATEGIES

Purpose To have a list ready of nonharmful coping strategies to refer to during difficult times.

List below all the helpful and nonharmful coping strategies you can think of, including those in Exercise 3.3. You do not have to be using these strategies currently to list them here. Ask other people what they do to cope with feeling bad, and list the strategies here if you think they are useful and nonharmful.

Nonharmful coping strategies

_____

_____

_____

_____

_____

_____

_____

_____

_____

_____

Example

Wakefield Survivors's Group positive/nonharmful coping strategies

Taking things one step at a time
Writing a letter
Taking a time out
Taking care of yourself
Talking/sharing your feelings
Ripping up an old phone book
Massage/body work
Respecting and loving yourself
Hitting/thumping/throwing objects without hurting yourself
Going to the doctor and getting more help and advice

Seeing it as it was
Meditation
Laughing
Playing
Healing tears
Dancing
Singing
Walking
Pausing/delaying—finding out what you are feeling and who you are feeling it about

> **Survivor's comment**
>
> It was easy to complete this from my list in Exercise 3.3, but it was hard to ask others how they coped. I found people I trusted and respected to add things to my list. —*Rebecca*

Strengthening Your Use of Nonharmful Coping Strategies

During the next week, try to use the nonharmful coping strategies on your list. To begin using nonharmful coping strategies and to maintain their use, you need to become aware of the problems you are having on a regular basis and the coping strategies you are using.

It can be tempting to return to old, familiar ways of coping. Notice when you are doing this. If possible, substitute a nonharmful coping strategy at least once during the week. Gradually begin to use ways of expressing and processing your feelings instead of blocking or distracting yourself.

Sometimes you may need to block or distract to stop yourself from feeling overwhelmed and to give yourself a "time out" from this work. Try to use the least harmful strategy in this case. Don't worry if you use old harmful coping strategies—it does not mean you have failed. At this stage, you're trying to become aware of *what* you are doing and *why* you are doing it. Actually changing old habits takes longer. Coping strategies that have become problems in their own right, such as alcohol or drug use, eating disorders and self-harm, may require professional help to change. But it is never too soon to try making some changes, however small.

EXERCISE 3.5 MONITORING COPING STRATEGIES

Purpose   To help you focus on the kinds of coping strategies you are using currently as a first step to increasing the use of helpful, nonharmful strategies.

During the next week, fill in the table below. Each day, record any difficult feelings or problems you experience in column 1. In column 2, record the coping strategies you used to try to deal with each of these difficulties. Record all your attempts to deal with your difficulties, whether they are harmful or harmless. Try to fill in this chart as close as possible to the time you experienced the problem. You might want to make copies of the table before you fill it in so that you can repeat this exercise from time to time while you are working through this book.

	Difficulty	Coping strategies
Examples	Had a fight. Felt angry and upset	Binged on chocolate. Phoned a friend
Monday		
Tuesday		
Wednesday		
Thursday		
Friday		
Saturday		
Sunday		

Rebecca's example

	Difficulty	Coping strategies
Monday	Major problems at work. Felt afraid and vulnerable	Withdrew. Took extra medication. Inadequate eating. Got a massage

(continued)

	Difficulty	Coping strategies
Tuesday	Yesterday's problems continued. Felt afraid and vulnerable, also angry and responsible	Talked about it with my therapist. Put problems into perspective. Hugged my purple pillow (my safety object)
Wednesday	Feeling frightened and stressed	Talked to colleagues and boss about the situation and gained their support. Tried to shut off how I had handled the situation. Came close to "shut down" (nonfunctioning) but knew this wasn't the answer. It would only have made the problem worse
Thursday	Anxious because work not done for tomorrow. Angry that other things led to distraction and now I had to do it on my day off	Wrote down how I felt. Planned action I needed to take. Did it and sacrificed day off to reduce anxiety
Friday	Felt inadequate as a professional and a person	Made a list of feelings about my job and put them into fact and fiction columns—that way I could see exactly what was true and what I imagined. Then distracted myself
Saturday	No real difficulty	
Sunday	Felt beaten and tired	Finished this exercise. Reviewed earlier affirmation writings and realized how much better things were

Survivor's comment

It helped me look logically at a problem instead of catastrophizing. It also helped me identify individual feelings whereas I often just have a blanket depressed feeling. As the week went on, I felt more enlightened and slowed down. I kept on completing the exercise and it helped me see reality. I think it will help me to focus on using positive coping mechanisms when troubles arise.   —*Rebecca*

Giving Yourself Positive Experiences

When we feel very depressed, fearful or confused, remembering the things we usually do that make us happy or at least help to maintain us on an even keel can be hard. We need to make sure that we do some of the things that will help maintain our well-being every day.

EXERCISE 3.6
GIVING YOURSELF POSITIVE EXPERIENCES

Purpose   To make sure you give yourself positive experiences and start the day in a positive frame of mind by reminding yourself that there are things that give you pleasure.

1) Each morning when you wake up, before you have opened your eyes, think of three things that you will do today that you will like. They don't have to be big things. They can be small, everyday things; for example, drinking a cup of coffee, taking a bath or watching your favorite TV show.
2) When you are in a good mood, write a list below of ten things that give you pleasure. Try to do one of these things each day.

Ten Things I Enjoy

-
-
-
-
-

-
-
-
-
-

Example

Annabelle's list of pleasurable experiences

Pick flowers   Take a day trip on the train
Read a book   Tune in to a different radio channel

(continued)

Go for a walk or swim   Enroll in a night class
Go to the movies   Paint my toenails
Do a crossword   Go to bed early
Plant some flower bulbs   Rent a movie
Buy a plant   Make a picnic and go out for the day

In this chapter we have tried to help you learn more about the strategies you use to cope with the effects of being abused. You may be using blocking strategies that are harmful or have become problems in their own right. We hope you can now try to use more of the nonharmful coping strategies to understand, express and process your experiences.

Taking care of yourself, and thinking about and doing things you enjoy, are also positive ways to help you cope. At times you may feel that you still need to use old, harmful coping strategies. This does not mean you have failed or have gone back to "square one." It takes time to change long-term habits, especially if they feel familiar and safe. In the next chapter, we continue to help you cope with your problems by looking at how memories and feelings are triggered, and what you can do about this.

4

Dealing with Emotions, Flashbacks and Hallucinations

Sexual abuse is a traumatic experience that for some is repeated over and over. Children can find this experience so overwhelming that they can't process it or come to terms with their thoughts and feelings about what is happening. As adults, survivors can continue to be troubled by such unprocessed memories and feelings. They may feel continually flooded and overwhelmed, or they may try to cope by blocking their feelings. In the last chapter we looked at the many coping strategies that can be used to block thoughts and feelings.

Pushing away memories and feelings can be useful and necessary at times. However, one difficulty with this strategy is that many things might remind you of your abuse, and you may not always be able to avoid these things. Survivors who try to push away their memories and feelings are vulnerable to being suddenly reminded of the abuse. This can result in extreme emotional states, flashbacks and hallucinations.

This chapter helps you learn more about what triggers emotional states, flashbacks and hallucinations, and to find ways of gaining some control over these experiences. To overcome these symptoms, you will need to continue to work on the underlying trauma—the sexual abuse itself—but for now you may be able to get a little more control over what can be frightening and confusing experiences.

Extreme Emotional States, Flashbacks and Hallucinations

Extreme Emotional States

Extreme emotional states can result when memories of past experiences are triggered. Painful feelings may come flooding back. Survivors frequently describe suffering panic attacks, bouts of depression, fits of rage or floods of tears for no apparent reason. Your feelings may take you by surprise. You may be unable to understand where they are coming from and what they are about. You may not feel much about your own abuse, but you may weep profusely at a film or book, or be outraged at an injustice that has been done to another person. You may find yourself being angry at people for what appears on the surface to be trivial reasons.

Flashbacks

Flashbacks are vivid memories in which a person feels he or she is re-experiencing past events. During a flashback, the survivor feels as if he or she is a child again and is reliving the abuse. Flashbacks are one way in which blocked feelings and memories surface. They can happen at any time or anywhere, but are usually triggered by reminders of the abuse.

> While I was having sex with my husband, he suddenly became the abuser. I pushed him away and jumped out of bed in fear. This was the first time my husband experienced me having a flashback.   —Jean

Hallucinations

Many survivors we have worked with have told us about experiencing the presence of their abuser when the person could not possibly be there. They see their abusers, hear them (often making threats), smell them, sense their presence or feel themselves being abused again.

> I would see my abuser walking toward me with that look in his eyes that told me what he was going to do. I would want to hide in a corner to get away from him. Sometimes I could not see him but I could smell him—the smell on him of the factory where he worked.   —Jean

Survivors who have these kinds of hallucinations have often been strongly threatened about the consequences of disclosing the abuse.

> My abuser died in 1979, but he had always told me he could come back. After his death, I saw him lots of times, and I was convinced he had kept his word because he wanted me to keep quiet about the abuse.   —Jean

When survivors experience hallucinations, they believe their abuser is really with them in the present and continues to have control over them. This is obviously a very frightening experience. It can also be frightening to see, hear or feel your abuser when you know he or she cannot possibly be there. Survivors sometimes hallucinate other things also.

The first hallucination happened when I was washing myself. When I looked in the mirror, I began to see worm-like things crawling under my skin. At the time I was horrified and the fear was overwhelming. It got to the point where I would never look at myself in a mirror, and my wife had to remove all the mirrors in the house. I believed that my deceased abuser was doing this to make me go insane as a punishment for revealing details of my past. I also sometimes hear my name being called. —*Graham*

Many survivors think they are going mad and are too frightened to tell anyone about their experiences. This kind of experience is not unusual for survivors. People who have experienced other traumas, such as bereavement, also sometimes experience hallucinations.

Extreme emotional states, flashbacks and hallucinations can be extremely frightening and undermine your ability to cope. That is why it is important to find ways to understand and control these experiences. The first step is to understand more about what triggers these experiences. The next exercise helps you to do this.

Identifying Triggers

A trigger is anything that reminds you of your abuse or brings up feelings associated with the abuse. Triggers often operate out of our awareness or on the edge of our awareness. Triggers can come through any of our senses:

- **Hearing**—for example, words, accents, music
- **Vision**—for example, people, places, clothes, objects
- **Smell**—for example, cigarette smoke, aftershave
- **Touch**—for example, materials, physical contact
- **Taste**—for example, alcohol

EXERCISE 4.1 IDENTIFYING TRIGGERS

Purpose To identify what triggers emotional states, flashbacks and hallucinations for you.

1) Below is a list of common triggers to emotional states, flashbacks and hallucinations. If you feel up to it, take a quick look through this list. Some of the words may disturb you, and you may find that reading the list acts as a trigger to memories and feelings. If you begin to experience problems or feel you cannot cope, move on to part 2 of the exercise.

Common triggers

Words

Parts of the body
> For example, breast, cock, cunt, bottom

Relationship of the abuser to you
> For example, father, mother, grandfather, brother, aunt

Sexual words
> For example, sex, suck, fuck

Phrases

I love you
I'm not going to hurt you
You like this, don't you?
Daddy's little girl
Good boy

Smells

Tobacco
Alcohol
Aftershave
Engine oil
Grass
Sweat

Sexual behaviors

Oral sex
Masturbation
Certain sexual positions
> For example, someone on top of you

Anal intercourse
Types of touch
> For example, stroking

Kissing
Being looked at

Clothes

Jeans
Shorts
Bathrobe
Pajamas
Underwear
Uniforms
Clothes made of certain material
> For example, polyester, nylon, silk, cotton

Places

Bathroom
Bedroom
Garden shed
The house/place where you were abused
The town where you were abused

People

Your abuser
Children
Someone who looks like your abuser

Situations

Arguments
Feeling trapped
Feeling rejected
Feeling powerless
Feeling betrayed
Feeling ignored/unheard

Someone who has the same job/
role as your abuser
>   For example, minister,
>   doctor, caretaker
Someone who acts or talks in
>   the same way as your abuser

Other

Glazed eyes

False teeth

Nakedness

Pubic hair

A certain day of the week

A certain time of the year
>   For example, Christmas

Photographs

Weather
>   For example, wind,
>   rain, sun

Certain tastes

Tickling

Sitting next to someone

A certain time of day, such as
>   evening

Certain types of music

Alcohol

Drugs

Chocolate

Media reports of abuse

Lack of sleep

2) Under each heading below, write down anything that you *know* is a trigger for you, or that you think *might* be a trigger for you. Use the list above to help you. You will probably think of other triggers that aren't included here. Write them down if you can, but don't worry if that is too hard right now. Keep the list, and as you become aware of other triggers, write those down too.

Words

Phrases

Smells

Sexual behaviors

(continued)

Clothes   **Places**

People   **Situations**

Other

Jean's example

Words   **Phrases**
Abuse   I love you
Rape   Do you love me?
Dad   Favorite little girl
Secret   Can you keep a secret?
Sex   Do you like it?
Bathroom

Smells   **Sexual behaviors**
Cigarettes   Touching (breast, vagina)
Factory smell   Being stared at
Sweat   Sometimes just touching
Beer   (hugging, putting arms
                                    around shoulder)

Clothes   **Places**

Short skirts
Low-cut tops
Swimwear

Bathroom
Bedroom

People
Sisters
Brothers
Someone who looks like my
    abuser or mother

Situations
Being trapped in a confined
    space with men
Parents kissing daughters
Going to the women's
    restroom when the men's is
    next door and a man goes in

Other
Drunks
Photos of when I was little
Getting dressed/undressed
    in front of my husband
Watching love scenes on TV

Friends talking about their
    childhood
Hearing about abuse on
    TV/radio
Strangers (men) sitting
    next to me

Survivors' comments

I hadn't realized how many things started thoughts in my mind and caused a lot of fears about my abuse. —Jean

This exercise made me think, and I felt my mind was more organized when I reread it. Stick with it. It does work. Try it and see. —Maya

It was good to recognize what I think triggers me. I still couldn't write down some of the triggers because they reminded me of the abuse. I made a decision not to write down the really hard stuff. I made a mental note of them so I could deal with them later. Only do what feels comfortable. Hang the list somewhere private and add to it over several weeks. —Rebecca

I didn't realize until now how having my feelings ignored in the present makes me extremely angry. —Catherine

I started to remember things I had blocked out. You need to be prepared for this. —Lesley

Do not rush the exercise. Think about it carefully. Keep returning to the exercise as more things become apparent. —Coral

For years my husband did the ironing because if I did it, I'd feel miserable and anxious and become absorbed in the unhappy relationship I have with my father. Then I had a flashback in which my father had come into my bedroom with his shirt over his head and sleeves flapping, pretending to be a ghost. In another flashback, I was raped while putting freshly laundered sheets and shirts away in the closets. This made me realize where the anxiety was coming from. I was trying to protect myself from being abused like that again, but I no longer need to be on full alert. So now I have no excuse for avoiding the ironing!   —Annabelle

Monitoring Triggers

It can be difficult sometimes to identify triggers to emotional states, flashbacks and hallucinations. The triggers might be things you have reacted to so often, or so suddenly, that you aren't aware of what they are. The exercises in this chapter are intended to bring the triggers back into your awareness.

Keep trying to identify the triggers. Try to think back to the point just before you had a flashback or hallucination or started to feel bad. Recall what happened next:

- Where were you?
- What could you see, hear, smell, feel and taste?
- What people were around?
- What was said and done?
- What were you thinking about?

If you were watching the TV or listening to the radio, recall what was happening in the program you were watching or listening to.

Thoughts that act as triggers can be difficult to identify because we are constantly thinking and running a commentary on whatever we are doing. Certain trains of thought may have happened so frequently that they become automatic; that is, you are thinking things without being too aware of what you are thinking. These automatic thoughts are important because they can have a profound effect on how you feel. However, when you are not aware of your automatic thoughts, it may seem as if your feelings have come "out of the blue."

You may experience a panic attack or sense of dread. You might feel weak and start trembling. This happens for a reason—train yourself to identify the trigger. You might have seen someone who looks like your abuser and it hasn't registered. You might have seen a little girl crying and you start to shake and want to cry and run away. You might have seen a particular chocolate bar in a store and you feel sick or sexy. Make yourself stop, concentrate and go back to look carefully for the trigger. Next time you may not be affected or the trigger will be much less potent. —*Annabelle*

EXERCISE 4.2 MONITORING TRIGGERS

Purpose To focus daily on what is triggering your emotional states, flashbacks and hallucinations as a first step toward controlling these experiences.

During the next week, fill in the table below. Each day, record any bad feelings, flashbacks or hallucinations you experience in column 1. In column 2, record what you think triggered these experiences. Try to fill this in as near as possible to the time you experienced the problem. Before you start, you might want to make copies of these pages so that you can repeat this exercise from time to time while you are working through this book.

	Bad feeling, flashbacks, hallucinations	Trigger
Examples	Flashback to being abused at age 7 Felt anxious	Having sex with my partner on top Friends talking about their childhoods
Monday		
Tuesday		

(continued)

	Bad feeling, flashbacks, hallucinations	Trigger
Wednesday		
Thursday		
Friday		
Saturday		
Sunday		

Maya's example

	Bad feeling, flashbacks, hallucinations	Trigger
Monday	Felt hurt, rejected, a failure as a mother	Not being invited to my daughter's going-away party
Tuesday	Felt left out, snubbed, upset	Saw a friend with someone else and she ignored me
Wednesday	Felt anxious, insecure	Argued with my husband about children

Thursday	Fear, worry. Flashback to abuse at a young age	A little girl who was playing alone outside. She chatted to me and told me her mother was at work
Friday	Fear, dread, guilt, anger. Flashback to finding out my children had been abused while I was having a barbecue and enjoying myself	My husband was using the barbecue
Saturday	Envy. Flashback of unfair treatment from my mother. Upset and confused	Visited a friend and her mother who have a good relationship. Good atmosphere, light-hearted conversation
Sunday	Sad, tearful. Regressed to a young age. Felt sorry for myself. It's not fair	Lying in bed thinking, "Sundays are family time"

Survivors' comments

I didn't want to spend a week focusing on bad feelings and flashbacks, but I knew if I wrote it down, I would feel better. It helped me see what was happening and it was therapeutic. I did pleasurable things during the week also. —*Maya*

I suddenly felt sad today, and I sat and thought about why that was. I was walking my dog, and I saw a couple with five children playing games with them. This started me thinking about my childhood. I can't remember going out with my parents and my sisters and brother, playing football or any other playground games as a family. Hurt and pain is all I remember as a child growing up. I remembered the exercises and the triggers that can cause flashbacks, etc. When I think about it, so many things in life hold memories like the family in the playground—chopping cabbage, hearing certain songs, making a mistake when I am driving in my car. —*Jean*

Dealing with Triggers

Identifying your triggers may, by itself, lessen the effect they have on you.

> Sometimes I'd be filled with dread. Then I'd look for the trigger that I had subconsciously registered. Once I had identified it—a little girl in the street, a man smoking a pipe, a graveyard—I seemed to become immune and it wouldn't bother me any more. At one time I reached a point where it was almost impossible to go to work because I had become so nervous driving and shook with dread and anxiety along a particular route. Then I looked at a map of the route, and there it was! Every morning I had to stop at a crosswalk and adjacent to it was a street with the same name as the one I'd lived on as a child. Once I realized that, the panic stopped.   —Annabelle

Working on your past abuse by using this book can help you understand and process your experiences and feelings, and you will be less likely to suffer sudden emotional states, flashbacks and hallucinations. In the meantime, however, you may also need to find other ways of dealing with the triggers themselves. Below we discuss two ways of doing this—by avoiding them and by using coping strategies.

Avoidance

Some triggers are easily avoided without changing your life too much.

- **Long-term avoidance.** If, for example, you are getting flashbacks during sex and you can identify that the triggers are certain positions, acts, types of touch or words that your partner is saying, you could ask your partner not to do or say these things. Think of different things you can do and say to each other that don't remind you of the abuse.
- **Short-term avoidance.** There may be triggers that you would not want to avoid in the long term but could avoid in the short term as a means of stabilizing your feelings and experiences and gaining a sense of control. Jean found that she often became upset and tearful when trying to relax in the evening and watch TV. She realized that there were often stories about children being abused in movies and dramatic series that she was watching and that this was triggering her bad feelings. She decided to avoid watching anything about child abuse by turning off the TV or going into another room. Jean

hopes this will only need to be a short-term strategy until she feels confident that she can watch these programs without being badly affected.

EXERCISE 4.3 AVOIDING TRIGGERS

Purpose   To help you identify ways in which you could avoid some of your triggers to extreme emotional states, flashbacks and hallucinations.

Under the left-hand column below, list any triggers that you think you can avoid without it interfering with your life too much. In the right-hand column, write a plan of how you will avoid the trigger.

Triggers that could be avoided   **How to avoid**

_____   _____

_____   _____

_____   _____

_____   _____

_____   _____

_____   _____

_____   _____

_____   _____

_____   _____

_____   _____

Examples

Triggers that could be avoided   **How to avoid**

Maya

Staying in bed and feeling depressed. Feeling panicky because I don't have enough time to get things done. Feeling like a failure

Make a list of things to do; e.g., get up at 9 A.M. Plan a morning timetable to get work done. Do something enjoyable in the afternoon as a reward

(continued)

Lesley

Having sex with my partner on top	Find a position that I feel safe in
Seeing my brother	Not going past his house
Certain foods	Do not buy them
Wedding dresses	Do not look at wedding dresses. I won't get married in one

Coral

Certain types of music	Change radio stations to one that is unlikely to play this type of music
Smoky rooms	Open the window
Having photo taken	Don't go places where I am likely to have my photo taken. Tell people I don't want to have my photo taken

> **Survivor's comment**
>
> It made me think about getting out or away from the trigger. Normally I would stay in the situation—I saw this as my punishment. It is going to be hard to put this coping strategy into action but I will try.   —Jean

Using Coping Strategies

Avoiding the things that trigger difficult feelings and experiences is one way to cope. However, you probably can't avoid all your triggers without severely restricting your life. Once you become aware of what your triggers are, you can start to find other ways of coping. Look back at the nonharmful coping strategies you identified in Exercise 3.4 and think of using one of these coping strategies after a trigger has occurred. Relaxing, challenging thoughts that something terrible will happen, or using one of your nonharmful coping strategies after you have become aware of a trigger, can stop you from going into extreme emotional states or having flashbacks and hallucinations. After the exercise below, we suggest some strategies particularly designed to deal with flashbacks and hallucinations.

EXERCISE 4.4 USING COPING STRATEGIES TO DEAL WITH TRIGGERS

Purpose   To help you identify coping strategies to deal with your triggers.

List five triggers below that you encounter frequently. For each trigger, identify the type of coping strategies you could use in response. Your coping strategies may be different depending on where the trigger occurred; for example, at home or in a public place.

Trigger	Coping strategy

Example

Someone sitting next to me on the sofa	Tell myself the abuse is in the past and I am safe now. Try to relax. Write down my thoughts and feelings later

Trigger	Coping strategy

_____   _____

_____   _____

_____   _____

_____   _____

_____   _____

_____   _____

_____   _____

_____   _____

_____   _____

Examples

Trigger	Coping strategy

Maya

Being presented with a plateful of food that my husband cooked especially for me	Tell my husband it triggers bad feelings. Say I don't want him to cook food especially for me. Write down feelings/flashbacks. Tolerate him sulking and feeling hurt without taking responsibility for it. Do something else, such as listen to relaxing music, exercise

(continued)

Trigger	Coping strategy
Being on my own with a man; for example, a patient at work	Explain to a colleague, and work together where possible. Walk out of the room on pretext of getting records, equipment, etc. Slow down breathing. Have a plan of what to do if he makes a sexual remark or tries to touch me; for example, say, "That is not why you are here. You are here for a physical exam, and that's it." Refuse to continue if the bad behavior continues. Call the police

Anthony

Passing the home of my abuser and the house where the abuse took place	Take a different route (avoid). Tell myself that the abuse is in the past and will not happen to me again

Jean

Smell a strong smell. (Sometimes I think this is the abuser coming to get me and it causes a hallucination)	Check out where the smell is coming from. Tell myself, "Don't let your imagination run away with you."

Survivor's comment

This exercise helped me prepare and gave me a plan. I wrote out coping strategies and felt more positive and calmer and could think more clearly. The exercise was empowering and it brought back memories of how healing it was to write. This is very positive stuff. —*Maya*

Dealing with Flashbacks and Hallucinations

Having a flashback or a hallucination is not necessarily a problem. The problem lies in the terror and powerlessness you experience because you believe you are a child again, that the abuse is happening again or the abuser is really present. To lessen this fear and help you feel more in control, try to stay in contact with the reality that you are an adult, that the abuser isn't really present and that you are re-experiencing things that happened in the past but aren't happening now. The goal at this stage is to help you overcome your fear of flashbacks and hallucinations, not necessarily to stop them. Below we discuss ways to help you do this.

Grounding Exercises

Grounding exercises help bring your focus back into the present.

- Focus on your breathing. Breathe slowly in through your nose and out through your mouth.
- Become aware of what is under your feet and your hands; for example, the carpet under your feet, the wood of the chair arms under your hands.
- Make physical contact with an object associated with the present time. Keep an object with you that can act as a reminder that you are now an adult—choose an object that you did not have as a child. A ring, a bracelet, car keys or any object that will be easily accessible to you at all times is best.
- Hearing someone else's voice can help you keep a link with the present. If there is anyone with you, ask him or her to keep talking to you—it doesn't matter what the person says, although reminding you where you are and how old you are helps. Follow the advice on reality orientation below.

EXERCISE 4.5 REALITY ORIENTATION

Definition *Reality orientation* is about reminding yourself of your present situation as a way of understanding that you are no longer a child who is being abused. This helps stop flashbacks and bring you back to the present. It can also help to use this after you have completed other exercises in this book, or if you feel you are regressing to a child-like state.

Purpose To help you bring yourself back to present reality when you are about to have a flashback or you are having a flashback.

Get a small card, such as an index card, and copy sentences 1 to 6 below, filling in the blanks. If you live at the address where you were abused, skip sentence 3. If you live with the person who abused you as a child or with any of the people you see in your flashbacks, skip sentence 4. Keep this card with you at all times, and if you are about to have a flashback, get it out and read it. Write down the answers again if you can.

1) My name is _____.

2) I am _____ years old.

3) I live at (write your address) _____.

4) I live with _____.

5) I work as _____.

6) I have _____ children. They are called _____.

Copy sentences 7 to 10 below and keep a copy with you at all times. Every time you are about to have a flashback, get out this paper and answer the following questions. Write down the answers if you can. Write down where you are and what you can see, hear and touch *in reality*. Don't write down the flashback.

7) I am in/at (where you are) _____.

8) I can see _____.

9) I can hear _____.

10) I can touch _____.

Example

1) My name is *Jenny Shaw.*

2) I am *37* years old.

3) I live at *1710 Smithfield Road, Anytown.*

4) I live with *my partner and children.*

5) I work as *a part-time secretary.*

6) I have 2 children. They are called *Ben and Patty.*

7) I am in/at *my living room.*

8) I can see *my TV, my easy chair, the photographs of my children, my houseplants.*

9) I can hear *the radio in the kitchen, the traffic outside.*

10) I can touch/feel *the carpet underneath my feet, the arms of the couch, the bracelet I bought two months ago.*

Dealing with Flashbacks

Below are ten steps to help you deal with flashbacks. Photocopy this page or copy the steps on an index card and keep it with you at all times. When you feel a flashback coming, read the steps below and act on them. If you know someone you trust who would be willing to help you, prepare the person in advance for what might happen by explaining to him or her about flashbacks. Ask this person to help you work through these steps when you are having a flashback.

During the flashback
  1) **Recognize and name what is happening.**
     "I'm having a flashback."
  2) **Tell someone else what is happening.**
     Even if you are not with people who know how to help you, it is worth telling them that you need time and space to deal with what is happening to you.
  3) **Remind yourself that the worst is over.**
     For example, "This isn't happening now, even if it feels like it. I'm remembering something that happened years ago. It's over."
  4) **Breathe slowly, focus on your breathing and ground yourself.**
  5) **Re-orient yourself to the present.**
     Use Exercise 4.5 above.
  6) **Remind yourself that you are an adult.**
     Remind yourself that you are an adult now, and try to calm and reassure the part of you that is frightened and feels as if you are a child.

After the flashback
  7) **Take time to recover.**
     Flashbacks can be emotionally and physically exhausting. Take time to recover—rest and be kind to yourself.
  8) **Write down what happened in the flashback.**
     The content of your flashback might provide useful information about what is still bothering you and what you are still having difficulty coming to terms with.
  9) **Identify what triggered the flashback and write it down.**
     Look back at Exercises 4.1 and 4.2.
 10) **Learn from it.**
     Although having a flashback can be very frightening, it is not a sign of failure but an experience you can learn from and use. Could you have done anything differently?

Survivors' comments

I used to think flashbacks were my way of punishing myself. Now I realize it happens to other people. By writing your flashbacks down you can break the hold your abuser has on you.   —Jean

1) Get your partner to ask you questions. Tell them not to be put off if you answer, "I don't know," or "I can't remember." It helps me if my partner says, "I'll count to three slowly and then you tell me what is bothering you."
2) Sometimes you might feel very anxious/depressed/agitated in the days or weeks before a particularly nasty memory comes up. Be aware of this.
3) Let yourself draw/write. Let the pen take over. Don't try and control your thoughts.
4) Keep a diary of dreams and flashbacks.   —Annabelle

I was sick of being tortured by flashbacks and sick of harming myself. I am now learning to function as a competent adult, instead of being so helpless and out of control.   —Maya

It is so frightening at the beginning, you feel that you are reliving the abuse all over again. You have to be strong, and the flashbacks do get easier to deal with. I try to put my mind on nice things rather than whatever is reminding me of the abuse. I also found that it helped me a lot to let a friend who understands talk to me. I am more in control of my flashbacks now.   —Lesley

Dealing with Hallucinations

We have worked with many survivors who have suffered from hallucinations of their abusers. Over time they managed to gain control of these experiences and eventually, by working on their past abuse, the hallucinations stopped. It is essential to this process that you work on your feelings toward your abuser, overcome fears about the consequences of speaking out, and realize that your abuser no longer has power and control over your life. You will probably not be able to stop your hallucinations right now (in fact, they could become more frequent as you work your way through this book), but there are techniques you can try to help lessen your fear and to gain some control over these experiences. We discuss these techniques below. Try them and see what works for you.

- Throw something harmless, like a scrunched-up paper towel, through the hallucination—Survivors are often amazed to find that the hallucination disappears. This can help reduce your fears and increase your feelings of control and personal power. Always throw something light and harmless, not an object that could cause any damage. A paper towel works just as well as a hard object.

> I think the main thing is to be aware that, although it seems real, you can control it and you can be strong enough to say, "I'm going to stop this and put it into perspective." If you are hallucinating, build up courage and go and touch the hallucination or throw something at it or yell at it. If you touch it and it disappears, then you can see that it is not really there. You realize you are stronger and you have some control. —Yvonne

- Reasoning can also help challenge the reality of hallucinations. Ask yourself how old the abuser looks and what he or she is wearing. In hallucinations, abusers usually look the age they were when the abuse took place, maybe ten, twenty or thirty years ago, and are wearing the same clothes. By making these observations, you will be able to reason with yourself—"He looks like he's about thirty, but he's actually in his mid-fifties now, so he can't be really here. I'm creating this image because of the fear in my mind." Or, "My abuser is dead, so he can't be here."
- Remind yourself: "This has happened before. I've seen my abuser and really believed she was with me, but then realized that she couldn't have been."
- Instead of keeping your experiences secret, test their reality by sharing them with someone you trust and asking, "Can you see/hear that too?"

Some survivors have mixed feelings about trying to stop the hallucinations.

> I feel safe in some ways when I have a hallucination, because then I know where he is. I don't have to sit there and wonder when he will appear. —Jean

Think about whether you have any reasons for not wanting to stop the hallucinations.

Survivors' comments

The hallucinations are still with me, but they're not as frequent and they don't frighten me like they did at first. I have learned how to deal with them. I tend to disregard them when they appear and continue whatever I am doing. If they occur at night when it is dark and I see something odd, I will turn on the light and look. The hallucination will not be present when I turn on the light. It gives me a sort of power, or to be more precise, it gives me a sense of achievement.   —*Graham*

I am no longer scared of my mother, and I don't have the hallucinations anymore.   —*Graham* (5 months later)

When my father [the abuser] first died, and until recently, I really believed he was coming back from the dead to get at me. Now I'm beginning to think it's the fear in me that creates the image of him. I start thinking of all he said he could do. I imagine him being there, and the fear is so intense that I see him and believe he really is there. I am now building up a resistance to this fear.   —*Jean*

I used to smell my dad. He really had a strong hold on me. Now the hallucinations aren't as strong as they used to be. I see now that my mind conjured up an image of him that seemed so real. Now I accept that he can't come back. Because I'm watching out for triggers now, it's making me think how to deal with them and to think of the positives. I am stronger now and when I do see him, I tell myself he is not real, it is my imagination.   —*Jean* (2 months later)

Although it is possible to gain some control over your hallucinations by using these techniques and working through this book, many survivors will probably need to seek help from a therapist. Graham and Jean have both received therapy.

Make sure your therapist understands about trauma-based hallucinations and is willing to work with you on them. Not all therapists or mental health workers share this understanding of hallucinations, especially within psychiatry, and they may only be able to offer you medication. While medication can be helpful in alleviating symptoms, it is rarely a long-term answer to the kind of hallucinations suffered by survivors of sexual abuse that we have described here.

In Part 1 of this workbook, we have helped you look at how you have been affected by being abused and the strategies you use to try to cope, some of which may have become problems in their own right. The exercises in this chapter and the previous chapter help prepare you for the work in the rest of the workbook. The previous chapter helps you to look at ways of coping with memories and feelings and to move toward using coping strategies that won't cause additional problems. This chapter helps you become aware of what kinds of things trigger memories and feelings and to gain control over these experiences. We hope that these exercises have helped you gain more understanding of your feelings and behaviors and have helped prepare you for the work ahead. The next section of the book deals with issues of guilt and self-blame.

PART 2

Guilt and Self-Blame

Survivors often feel they are responsible for being sexually abused. Many survivors believe that somehow they caused the abuse to begin and that the abuse continued because they didn't stop it. Feeling guilty and blaming yourself for the abuse can undermine your self-confidence and prevent you from realizing your full potential.

Part 2 helps you understand more about feelings of guilt and self-blame and to place the responsibility for abuse with the abuser.

In chapter 5, you are asked to look at your beliefs that you are to blame because you didn't stop the abuse or tell anyone. Chapter 6 helps you explore beliefs that you may have caused the abuse to begin and helps you understand more about how abuse does happen. Chapter 7 looks at why some survivors find it difficult to let go of feelings of guilt and self-blame.

Why Didn't I Stop the Abuse?

This chapter begins by asking you to look at your current beliefs about who was responsible for the sexual abuse you experienced as a child. The rest of the chapter aims to help you challenge any thoughts that you were to blame because you didn't stop the abuse or tell anyone.

Many survivors have been abused by more than one person. If you have been abused by more than one person, repeat the exercises in this chapter for each of your abusers. You can photocopy the exercises, write out the exercises again or use a different color pen for each abuser.

The next two exercises help you rate the extent to which you are currently blaming yourself for the abuse. Photocopy or make a written copy of Exercises 5.1 and 5.2 so that you can repeat them at the end of chapter 8 and at other times while you are reading this book.

EXERCISE 5.1
RESPONSIBILITY CAKE

Purpose To identify the extent to which you think and feel that different people are responsible for the abuse you suffered.

It may help you complete this exercise if you first look at the example that follows it.

Date _____

1) Who sexually abused you? _____
   (If you were abused by more than one person, name one abuser each time you do the exercise.)
2) Write down the names of all the people you think or feel might be responsible in any way for your abuse. _____
3) Following is a circle or "cake." Divide the cake into slices to represent how much you *think* each of the people above was responsible for the abuse you suffered.

(continued)

How much I *think* each person was responsible for the abuse:

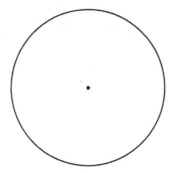

4) Now divide the cake below to show how much you *feel* each of the people above was responsible for your abuse.

How much I *feel* each person was responsible for the abuse:

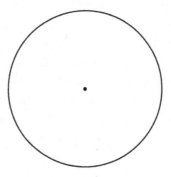

Note: You may find you divide the two cakes in different ways. For example, some survivors *know* (think) they are not responsible for the abuse, but *feel* that they are partly responsible.

Rebecca's example

Below is an example of Rebecca's responsibility cakes. As we can see from the first circle, Rebecca *thinks* her abuser is mostly responsible for the abuse, but she also blames herself and her mother. However, when we look at the second circle, we can see that she actually *feels* that she and her mother are more responsible for the abuse and feels her abuser has much less responsibility for what happened.

1) Who sexually abused you? *my dad*
2) Write down all the people you think or feel might be responsible in any way for your abuse. *me, mother, the abuser*

3) How much I *think* each person was responsible for the abuse:

4) How much I *feel* each person was responsible for the abuse:

> ### Survivor's comment
>
> While I was doing the exercise, I was constantly fighting the temptation to yet again accept all responsibility for my abuse. It helped me to see the difference between what I think/know to be true and what I feel. They are very different things that are often confused. —Rebecca

Beliefs about the Responsibility
for Sexual Abuse

We develop beliefs about ourselves in childhood as a result of our experiences and our interactions with other people. Often these beliefs remain unchanged throughout our lives. For example, if you were brought up to believe that it didn't matter how you felt, you may continue to believe this is true as an adult. This exercise asks you to look at your beliefs about who is responsible for sexual abuse and rate how strongly you believe them. Even though we may hold certain very strong beliefs, it does not mean they are true. The three chapters in this section help you to re-examine these beliefs as an adult to see how true they really are.

EXERCISE 5.2 BELIEFS ABOUT
THE RESPONSIBILITY FOR SEXUAL ABUSE

Purpose To look at your current beliefs about who is to blame for the abuse.

Look through the following list of beliefs. For each one, ask yourself, "How much do I believe this right now?" Choose the number that corresponds to how much you believe each one:

- If you don't believe it at all, circle 0.
- If you are unsure, circle 5.
- If you totally believe it, circle 10.

	Don't believe at all	*?*	*Totally believe*
I could not stop the abuse because the abuser had power over me	0 1 2 3 4	5	6 7 8 9 10
There are good reasons why I couldn't tell anyone	0 1 2 3 4	5	6 7 8 9 10
I was abused because an abuser had access to me, not because of anything I had done	0 1 2 3 4	5	6 7 8 9 10
Abusers are always responsible for abusing children	0 1 2 3 4	5	6 7 8 9 10
I know my abuser was responsible for abusing me	0 1 2 3 4	5	6 7 8 9 10
The abuse was definitely not my fault	0 1 2 3 4	5	6 7 8 9 10

If you had more than one abuser:

I had more than one abuserbecause several abusers had access to me	0 1 2 3 4	5	6 7 8 9 10
I had more than one abuser because I was in a vulnerable and unprotected situation	0 1 2 3 4	5	6 7 8 9 10

Why Didn't I Stop the Abuse?

Sexual abuse is a trap. The abuser may use physical strength, power and authority, tricks, threats, treats or manipulation to coerce the child into the abuse and to keep him or her silent. Sexual abuse almost always involves some form of relationship between the abuser and the child that is designed by the abuser to entrap the child and prevent him or her from stopping the abuse or telling anyone about it.

Children are often sexually abused over weeks, months or many years, and often feel guilty because they believe they should have been able to stop the abuse or have told someone about it. They may believe that the abuse was at least partly their fault because they "let" it go on for so long. For many survivors, the abuse continues after age eighteen and may extend into their twenties, thirties or later. This can add to feelings of guilt and self-blame. Adults often carry the same beliefs and feelings of self-blame and shame they had as children, and this can prevent them from talking about their abuse or seeking help to overcome their problems.

The exercises below help you explore the reasons you could not stop the abuse or tell anyone about it and to help you understand that you were not to blame for the abuse continuing over time.

Many of the following exercises ask you to think back to your childhood. Use the ideas in chapter 1 to keep safe and stay at the emotional distance from your past that allows you to think about what was happening then without becoming too distressed. Repeat the exercises for each abuser if you were abused by more than one person. In this chapter, complete the exercises starting with your first abuser, because you will be looking at why you couldn't stop the abuse when it first started and how this makes it even more difficult for you to stop it later.

The next three exercises explore the power abusers have over their victims. The purpose of the exercises is to help you see that children are not powerful enough to say "No" or physically stop an abuser themselves.

Power

Adult survivors often forget how powerless they were as children compared to their abusers. Abusers are often bigger than their victims, but physical size is only one type of power. They may be in a position of power because of their relationship or their role in the child's life; for example, parents have power over their children and schoolteachers have power over the children in their class.

Abusers can also create a position of power over children by blackmailing, threatening or emotionally manipulating them. These sources of power can be more important than physical strength in controlling children. It is therefore possible for children to abuse other children of a similar size by exerting their power through emotional manipulation or through their position or role in their victims' lives. For example, an older sister may manipulate her siblings, a teenage baby-sitter has power over the children in his or her charge and a child may bully or abuse a classmate. Abusers misuse their power to frighten or control their victims.

EXERCISE 5.3 POWER

Purpose   To think about the kinds of power your abuser had over you, to help you understand that you could not stop the abuse yourself.

1) What was your abuser's relationship to you?
   Abuser's name _____
   Relationship to you _____
   (For example, the relationship may be parent, neighbor, priest, brother or sister, teacher, family friend, other child, stranger, baby-sitter.)

2) What kind of person was he or she?
   (For example, kind, well-respected, stern, bossy, violent, loving, feared.)

   _____

   _____

   _____

   _____

   _____

   _____

   _____

3) Read through this list of the things that give abusers power over their victims and check any that apply to you:
   • You were told to obey adults.
   • The abuser was an adult and you were a child.

- You wanted the abuser to love you, so you wanted to please him or her.
- You loved the abuser and were scared of losing the relationship.
- The abuser was a bossy or bullying person and you were scared of him or her.
- The abuser was an older child.
- The abuser was ill or disabled and you felt sorry for him or her.
- The abuser was head of the family and told everyone what to do.
- The abuser was in a position of power over you (such as a teacher).
- The abuser was a respected person who was a powerful person in relation to adults as well (such as a priest).
- The abuser threatened or frightened you.
- The abuser was bigger and stronger than you.

Can you add any others?

-
-
-
-
-

Adults are believed and children are considered the ones who tell lies. —Rebecca

4) Write down the kinds of power or authority your abuser had over you. Think of your relationship with the abuser, his or her job, position in your community and personality, and include any of the examples from above that apply to you.

_____

_____

_____

_____

_____

_____

(continued)

5) Do you know of anyone else your abuser had power over?
This does not have to be someone the abuser was sexually abusive to. It may even include animals or pets to which the person was cruel.
If so—who?

_____

_____

_____

_____

_____

_____

_____

_____

Doing this exercise made me feel angry and sad because I realized how vulnerable I was. I told myself it is all right for me to feel this way.
—Jean

I Didn't Say "No"

Everyone was afraid of my mother. She was a very strong member of the family who was always right. I never, ever said "No" to her, I wouldn't dare. She knew I was scared of her. She never treated me like a child, and she acted as if I was her property.   —Graham

Many survivors blame themselves for the abuse because, like Graham, they didn't say "No" to their abusers. Graham was too scared of his mother to stand up to her. Other survivors have been in a similar position because of the power their abusers held over them. To say "No" to someone, you have to feel you have the power to do this and will be listened to. Children do not have this power in relation to their abusers. Even when children do say "No," abusers often ignore them or even punish children for trying to resist.

Physical Size of Victims and Abusers

When abuse begins, abusers are usually bigger and stronger physically than their victims. The purpose of the following exercises is to show you how difficult it would have been for you to stop an abuser who was bigger than you. The abuser may have been a similar size to you if the abuser was a child of a similar age or if you were a teenager when the abuse started. Remember, physical size is only one of the ways that abusers keep their victims trapped in abusive relationships.

EXERCISE 5.4 PHYSICAL SIZE OF VICTIMS AND ABUSERS

Purpose   To look at the difference in physical size between children and adults.

1) How old were you when the abuse began? _____ years.
   Think about a child, *not yourself,* of this age (this could be a child you know or an imaginary child) or look at a child of this age. Compare the child's size and strength with that of an adult. Who is physically bigger or stronger? _____
   Would it be physically possible for the child to stop the adult from abusing him or her? Yes? No?
2) Draw a picture of a child (not yourself) of the same age you were when the abuse began.
   Draw a picture of an adult. (Drawing stick people is fine.)

A child   An adult

Look at the difference in physical size.
Would it be physically possible for the child to stop the adult from abusing him or her? Yes? No?
3) Write down any thoughts or feelings that came up for you when you answered questions 1 and 2 above:

_____

_____

(continued)

_____

_____

_____

_____

Graham's example

A child   An adult

EXERCISE 5.5
PHYSICAL SIZE OF YOU AND YOUR ABUSER

Purpose To help you see how difficult it would have been for you, as a child, to physically stop the abuser.

 This exercise asks you to draw your abuser and yourself, and to look at photographs of your abuser and yourself as a child. If this feels too frightening for you, try using a distancing technique from chapter 1. For example, imagine you are looking at the photographs or drawings through the wrong end of a telescope to make them appear smaller and have a less powerful effect on you.

1) Draw a picture of yourself and the abuser at the time the abuse _began_—again, stick drawings are fine. You may have been much older when the abuse ended, but it is important that you draw yourself as you were when the abuse began.

Me   The abuser

Compare the difference in size between you as a child and the abuser in the drawings.

Would it have been possible for you to physically stop the abuser from abusing you? Yes? No?

2) Find a photograph of yourself at the age the abuse *began.*
Compare your size in the photograph with an adult or, if possible, with a photograph of your abuser.
Would it be possible for you to physically stop the adult from abusing you? Yes? No?

3) Note here any thoughts or feelings that come up for you:

_____

_____

_____

_____

_____

_____

Jean's example

This is me   My abuser

Jean was so terrified of her abuser that she exaggerated his size in her drawing. He was much bigger than she was, but her fear made him appear to her even bigger than he actually was.

I was a child. I was small. He was bigger than me. I was not strong enough to stop him.   —Lesley

I felt terror, sadness, confusion, hatred and anger. I was sweating. I wanted to pick the child up and cuddle her. The child needed help.
—Jean

Looking at the stick drawings of a child and an adult, I can see the adult is at least three times bigger. When I draw myself and one of my abusers (my mother), I can see she was bigger than me and a lot stronger, but I should have been able to stop the abuse when I was fifteen and bigger than my mother.   —Graham

After doing this exercise you may, like Graham, be able to see that when the abuse began you were too small to stop it, but you may still think you should have been able to stop the abuse when you were older and bigger. Male survivors often feel especially ashamed because they think they should have been physically strong enough to stop their abusers, particularly when they became teenagers. Survivors of either sex may think they should have been strong enough to stop abuse by women. Remember that physical strength is only one form of power that abusers hold over their victims. When abuse has gone on for some time, you become trapped by the abuser's emotional power and manipulation, and this can prevent you from even beginning to think about how to protect yourself.

Why Children Don't Tell

After completing the exercises above, you may begin to see the ways your abuser had power over you and perhaps over other children or adults. The power that abusers hold over their victims makes it unlikely that children can stop the abuse themselves. The only other way children might be able to stop abuse is to tell an adult who would be willing and able to help. The majority of children do not feel able to talk to anyone about their abuse. There are many reasons for this, and the following exercises explore these reasons.

EXERCISE 5.6 WHY CHILDREN DON'T TELL

Purpose   To help you think about the reasons why children and teenagers are unable to tell anyone about sexual abuse.

If you have spent your life feeling ashamed and guilty about the abuse, it may be difficult to think about your own situation without being overwhelmed by your feelings. When you do this exercise, think about other children, of any age, who are being sexually abused.

Children feel many pressures to keep quiet about sexual abuse and there are many reasons why they can't tell. Spend some time thinking about the reasons why children can't tell anyone when they are being abused.

Thinking about the following may help you do this exercise:

- What is the child afraid of?
- Why might it be difficult to talk about sexual things?
- What is the child feeling?
- What is the child's understanding of what is happening?

Write below any reasons you can think of why children can't tell:

-
-
-
-
-
-
-
-
-
-
-
-
-
-
-
-

EXERCISE 5.7
WHY CHILDREN CAN'T TELL

Purpose   To increase your awareness of the reasons why you could not tell others about the abuse.

The list below gives some of the reasons why children can't tell others when they are being abused. Read through them and check any that applied to you. See if you can add any more.

Who to tell?	Applied to you?
Parents dead, ill, absent	_____
Parents involved in the abuse	_____
No trustworthy adult around	_____
No opportunity to talk alone with a trusted adult	_____
Caregivers do not listen	_____
Frightened of parents	_____
Parents discourage talk about sex	_____
No friends	_____
No one to tell	_____

What to say?	
Too young to talk	_____
Don't know how to describe what's happening	_____
Too embarrassed and ashamed to say what is happening	_____

Fears about the consequences of telling

1. Threats from the abuser

No one will believe you	_____
You will be put into a home/foster care	_____
You will not see your mother again	_____
The family will be split up	_____
Affection and love will be withdrawn	_____
Family and friends will reject you	_____
No one will want to marry you	_____

Fears about the consequences of telling	Applied to you?
Threatened or actual violence to you, your family or pets	_____
The abuser will commit suicide or be put in prison	_____

2. Fears about other people's reactions

No one will believe you	_____
Mother will feel guilty	_____
The family will be hurt	_____
Mother/father will be upset	_____
Mother will reject you	_____
Other people will think you are to blame	_____
Other people will think you are dirty, contaminated or disgusting	_____
You will be rejected and the abuser supported	_____

3. Fears for the abuser

The abuser will be hurt and rejected	_____
The abuser will be put in prison	_____
The abuser will get beaten up	_____
The abuser will commit suicide	_____

4. Fears that telling won't help

Nothing will change	_____
No one can stop it	_____
Events will get out of control	_____
Fear of the unknown	_____
Others seem to know anyway	_____
It might get worse	_____
The abuser is too powerful and can't be stopped	_____

The child's confusion

Feelings and thoughts that prevent children from telling include

Feelings of guilt and self-blame	_____
Feelings of shame and embarrassment	_____
Confusion—Is it really happening? Is it wrong?	_____

(continued)

The child's confusion	Applied to you?
Thinking the abuse is normal	_____
Not understanding what is happening	_____
Believing you are the only one this has ever happened to	_____
Feeling dirty, contaminated, polluted	_____
Feeling trapped by the secrecy	_____
Feeling you are being punished and deserve it	_____
Hoping the abuse won't happen again	_____
Blocking out all memories of the abuse	_____
Feeling sorry for the abuser	_____
Not wanting to betray the abuser by telling	_____
Feeling it's your fault because you took candy, money, toys or other rewards from the abuser	_____
Enjoying the sexual stimulation	_____
Enjoying the affection, warmth or closeness	_____
Thinking, "I didn't tell when it first happened, so how can I tell now?"	_____

Other fears:

_____   _____

_____   _____

_____   _____

_____   _____

_____   _____

_____   _____

_____   _____

There are many reasons why most children and young people who are being abused are unable to tell anyone about what is happening. Despite being under a lot of pressure to keep quiet at the time of the abuse, survivors usually grow up blaming themselves for keeping the abuse secret. You have indicated on the list above the reasons why you were unable to tell, and this may increase your awareness of the pressures that were on you to keep quiet. Survivors often find it helps them understand more about why they kept the secret to write their own account of why they couldn't tell.

EXERCISE 5.8
WHY I COULDN'T TELL

Purpose　To help you understand the pressures you were under to remain silent about the abuse.

Write an account of why you were unable to tell anyone about the abuse. Use your answers from the previous exercise to help you. If you don't want to write an account, find some other way of representing why you couldn't tell; for example, a cartoon strip or a spidergram (see Nina's example on the next page).

It might help to complete this exercise if you try to answer the following questions first.

- How old were you when the abuse first began?
- Who could you have told?
- How do you think other people would have reacted?
- What are the reasons you couldn't tell someone right away?
- What reasons prevented you from telling, when the abuse had been happening for some time?

Why I couldn't tell

Examples

Nina

Nina and her sister spent their childhood in a children's home. All the children in the home were sexually, physically and emotionally abused by the woman in charge of the home. This is why Nina didn't tell:

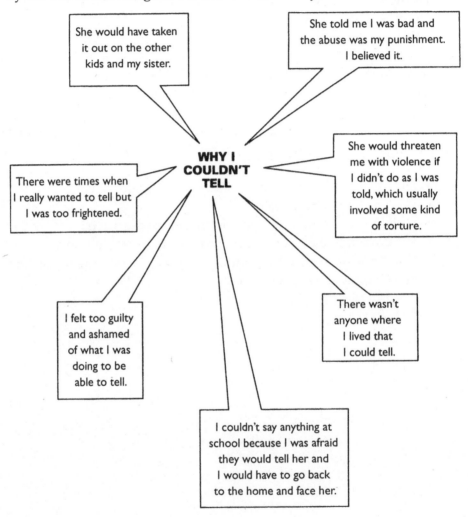

She would have taken it out on the other kids and my sister.

She told me I was bad and the abuse was my punishment. I believed it.

WHY I COULDN'T TELL

There were times when I really wanted to tell but I was too frightened.

She would threaten me with violence if I didn't do as I was told, which usually involved some kind of torture.

I felt too guilty and ashamed of what I was doing to be able to tell.

There wasn't anyone where I lived that I could tell.

I couldn't say anything at school because I was afraid they would tell her and I would have to go back to the home and face her.

Jonathan

I loved my grandma, she protected me from a very strict father. He could never understand why the grandmother of his five children chose to give me so much more in material things and love than she did the others. My father or brothers and sisters were always punishing me because they were jealous of the attention I got and said I was being spoiled by my grandmother. She started sexually abusing me when I was around three years old. She aroused me by hand and, as I got older, by mouth. When anybody told me how lucky I was to have such a wonderful grandma, I felt confused and in conflict. I didn't dare tell things that no one would believe. I felt like she had a control over my life that would never quit.

When I was fourteen years old, I couldn't stand it any more, so I ran away from home. I got a job at a fairground. I had to sleep in the back of a big furniture van where they kept the generator. There was no light, and the noise went on day and night. Two men who worked there forced me into the back of the van and pushed my face into a corner. One man kept his hand over my mouth while the other forced his body into me. The pain felt like I was being torn apart and I cried. I felt so degraded. I couldn't tell anyone I was raped, so I ran away again and went back home to a good hiding for causing so much worry. The rape and then the beating when I got home made me feel even more powerless. I couldn't do anything to stop the abuse. I could not reveal my secrets, so the abuse by my grandmother went on. My grandmother went to her grave with no one the wiser about her.

By giving Jonathan all her attention, Jonathan's grandmother effectively isolated him from the rest of the family, because they resented him for getting all of her "affection" and treats. It also made it unlikely that anyone would suspect that she was harming Jonathan, who appeared to be her favorite. Jonathan felt guilty because he enjoyed the presents and the attention he got, and this made him feel he was involved in the abuse. He also felt ashamed because, from a very early age, he responded sexually to her stimulating his penis.

Jonathan's unsuccessful attempt to escape the abuse by running away made him feel even more powerless to stop it. Looking at a photograph of himself when he was about five years old with his grandmother (Exercise 5.5) immediately made him realize that his grandmother was physically much bigger and stronger than he was at that time.

However, he was still very ashamed that the abuse by his grandmother continued until he left home at eighteen, because he knew he was physically strong enough by then to stop the abuse. His feelings of shame made it much harder for him to think about why the abuse had continued until he was in his late teens. He believed that as a young man he should have been able to stop an old woman from abusing him.

After looking back and reassessing the power she held over him, he began to understand how she had trapped him into the abusive relationship by confusing him and controlling his emotions. He became aware of her emotional power over him and how easy it was for her to manipulate him and the rest of his family. Jonathan's shame at his sexual response, his guilt at receiving all of her attention and his feelings of total powerlessness left him feeling there was no way out. By looking back as an adult on his situation as a boy and a teenager, and thinking about how he had been trapped, Jonathan was at last able to break away from his shame and guilt and begin a new life.

> The exercise made me think carefully about the *real* reasons, not the imagined reasons, for why I didn't tell. It was a relief to know I did have real reasons. —Rebecca

Who Would Have Listened?

Twenty years ago, very few people were aware that so many children are sexually, physically and emotionally abused, and the majority of people would probably not have listened to or believed children who tried to disclose. If you had tried to disclose at that time you probably wouldn't have been protected. Over the last twenty years, society's awareness of sexual abuse has increased gradually. Nowadays sexual abuse is talked about regularly on television and radio and written about in newspapers and magazines. This increased awareness makes it more likely that children will be listened to and believed in the future. However, many people won't listen to or believe children, and the pressures on children to keep the secret remain the same.

I Did Tell

In the past, children who did tell often received a negative reaction or were not protected. You may have told someone who ignored you, didn't believe you, blamed you, was angry with you or did nothing to stop the abuse. These negative reactions could have made you feel you were not worth protecting or increased your feelings of shame and powerlessness. If you told and the abuse continued, this may have increased your belief that the abuser could not be stopped and made it less likely that you would try to tell again. Children who disclose and receive negative reactions often retract their statements and say the abuse didn't really happen.

People react to disclosures in negative ways for many reasons. Some find it hard to believe that sexual abuse happens. Others have not dealt with their own childhood abuse or are frightened of the consequences of believing and supporting the survivor. Their negative responses are due to problems within themselves, not because you were not worth protecting. You should have been believed and protected. Chapter 9 explores why mothers or other caretakers don't always listen to children or protect them.

Children are not able to stop abuse themselves and are rarely able to tell anyone about what is happening. Understanding this can help you feel less responsible for the abuse, but can also make you aware of how vulnerable and powerless you were as a child. In chapter 7, we help you look at the power you have now as an adult. In the next chapter, we continue to explore your beliefs that you are responsible for the abuse by looking at the reasons children erroneously believe they caused the abuse to begin.

6

Did I Cause the Abuse?

Survivors often believe that they caused the abuse to start or that they were chosen for abuse because of something about them. These thoughts may not always be completely conscious, but they can lead to deep feelings of guilt and shame. This chapter helps you explore your beliefs about why the abuse began and to begin to see that the cause of the abuse lies within the abuser, not with you.

If you have been abused by more than one person, repeat the exercises in this chapter for each of your abusers, starting with the abuser that you feel easiest answering these questions about.

EXERCISE 6.1 DID I CAUSE THE ABUSE?

Purpose   To help you become more aware of why you think you caused the abuse to begin.

Below is a list of reasons why survivors sometimes think that they caused the abuse to happen, or why they think they were chosen to be abused. For each reason, check one of the four columns below. At the end of the list, add any other reasons you think you caused the abuse, or were chosen, and rate them in the same way.

	Doesn't apply to me	*Definitely means I'm to blame*	*Could mean I'm to blame*	*Doesn't mean I'm to blame*
I was				
Flirtatious	_____	_____	_____	_____
Naughty	_____	_____	_____	_____
Well developed	_____	_____	_____	_____
Bad	_____	_____	_____	_____

(continued)

	Doesn't apply to me	Definitely means I'm to blame	Could mean I'm to blame	Doesn't mean I'm to blame
Pretty	_____	_____	_____	_____
Ugly	_____	_____	_____	_____
The oldest	_____	_____	_____	_____
The youngest	_____	_____	_____	_____
The middle one	_____	_____	_____	_____
Quiet	_____	_____	_____	_____
Lively	_____	_____	_____	_____
Put on earth to be abused	_____	_____	_____	_____
Too loving	_____	_____	_____	_____
Not loving enough	_____	_____	_____	_____
I showed my underpants	_____	_____	_____	_____
I got into bed with the abuser	_____	_____	_____	_____
I got into the bath with the abuser	_____	_____	_____	_____
I cuddled the abuser	_____	_____	_____	_____
I sat on the abuser's knee	_____	_____	_____	_____
I gave out a sign to my abuser	_____	_____	_____	_____
I enjoyed getting attention from the abuser	_____	_____	_____	_____

Other reasons

_____   _____   _____   _____   _____

_____   _____   _____   _____   _____

_____   _____   _____   _____   _____

_____   _____   _____   _____   _____

_____   _____   _____   _____   _____

It did help me identify those things I still had doubts about even after having had therapy. I kept reminding myself that I knew I wasn't to blame, even if I felt I was. —Rebecca

Jean completed this exercise twice. The first time, she filled it in as she had been thinking as a child, showing that, for many reasons, she felt she definitely was to blame. The second time, she filled it in as the adult she is now and indicated that she felt just a few of the reasons "could mean I'm to blame." She says,

This exercise brought back memories I didn't want to remember. It took me a while to fill in. I kept putting the sheet down to get my composure back. Every time a bad memory came to me and I felt weepy, I gave myself at least half an hour away from the exercise. —Jean

EXERCISE 6.2 WOULD YOU BLAME A CHILD?

Purpose To highlight any differences in the way you judge yourself and others.

Think of a child, maybe your own child, a child of a friend or neighbor, or any child that you know or have seen. Imagine that the child tells about being sexually abused and says he or she caused it because of the reasons below. For each of the reasons the child gives, check one of the three columns to show how much you think that means the child is to blame for the abuse. Add your own reasons from the end of Exercise 6.1 and rate what you would think if the child gave you those reasons.

	The child is definitely to blame	The child could be to blame	The child isn't to blame
The child says he or she was			
Flirtatious	_____	_____	_____
Naughty	_____	_____	_____
Well developed	_____	_____	_____
Bad	_____	_____	_____
Pretty	_____	_____	_____
Ugly	_____	_____	_____
The oldest	_____	_____	_____
The youngest	_____	_____	_____

(continued)

	The child is definitely to blame	The child could be to blame	The child isn't to blame
The middle one	_____	_____	_____
Quiet	_____	_____	_____
Lively	_____	_____	_____
Fearful	_____	_____	_____
Put on earth to be abused	_____	_____	_____
Too loving	_____	_____	_____
Not loving enough	_____	_____	_____

The child says

I showed my underpants	_____	_____	_____
I got in bed with the abuser	_____	_____	_____
I got into the bath with the abuser	_____	_____	_____
I cuddled the abuser	_____	_____	_____
I sat on the abuser's knee	_____	_____	_____
I gave out a sign to my abuser	_____	_____	_____
I enjoyed getting attention from the abuser	_____	_____	_____

Other reasons

_____	_____	_____	_____
_____	_____	_____	_____
_____	_____	_____	_____
_____	_____	_____	_____

When you have done this, compare your answers to Exercise 6.1. Are you blaming yourself in ways you wouldn't blame this child? If so, explain why below.

_____

_____

_____

_____

_____

There is no way that I could imagine that an abused child could be given blame of any kind. This exercise let me put down on paper what I believed. I have given different answers to Exercises 6.1 and 6.2. I suppose I still judge myself much more harshly, not just with these questions but in day-to-day living. I expect a lot more from myself than I do from others, but I'm working on it! Try not to use your own situation when you do this exercise.   —Anita

I had difficulty not getting me and the child mixed up. I wanted to fill the exercise in as if it were me. I was getting upset about it and angry because of where I had to put the checkmarks. My feelings about being abused came to the forefront and about how I thought about myself. I had to keep remembering that the child I was thinking about was not me.   —Jean

This is a very important exercise. It enabled me to see the way we develop double standards in dealing with ourselves and others. We are always ready to blame ourselves. I felt angry that I was often too eager to take the blame and responsibility for things I had no control over. I am probably blaming myself because these were some of the reasons given to me by my abusers and by some of the people I sought help from. They were also some of the reasons I invented for being abused. I needed reasons for why I was treated like this.   —Rebecca

Finkelhor's Model: Four Steps before Abuse Occurs

In chapter 2, we look at Finkelhor's model about how abuse affects survivors. David Finkelhor (1984) has also studied the situations in which sexual abuse occurs and found that four things must happen before a child is abused:

1) There is a person who wants to abuse.
2) The person overcomes thoughts that abusing is wrong.
3) The abuser gets the child alone.
4) The abuser overcomes the child's resistance.

Understanding more about this model can help survivors challenge thoughts that they might have caused the abuse. You may feel angry or upset as you read more about the four steps below. Be prepared to have strong reactions and take a break when you need to.

1. There Is a Person Who Wants to Abuse

For sexual abuse to occur, first there must be a person who wants to abuse a child. This may sound obvious but, as we have seen, many survivors think the abuse started with themselves—their personality, appearance and behavior. Abuse does *not* start with the child; abuse starts with the thoughts and desires of a person who wants to abuse children.

It is still not clear why certain people want to abuse children. There are no simple answers to this question but it is probable that a number of factors are involved. What we do know is that a person doesn't come into contact with a certain child and suddenly become an abuser. Before the abuse occurs there is usually a period where the abuser fantasizes about what he or she is going to do to a child. The abuser's desire to abuse is not created by the child—it is there before the child appears.

Exercise 6.3 below lists factors that are thought might contribute to a person wanting to abuse. They are not excuses or justifications for abuse, and none of these factors in themselves explain why a person might abuse. For example, the majority of people who are abused as children do not go on to sexually abuse other people. Whatever the abuser's past experience, he or she is still responsible for the abuse. The problem lies within the abuser, not within yourself.

EXERCISE 6.3
WHY YOUR ABUSER WANTED TO ABUSE

Purpose   To help you understand that your abuser had a problem and was responsible for the abuse, not you.

Factors that might contribute to a person wanting to abuse
Check any of the following factors that you think might apply to your abuser. *Note:* You are unlikely to know much about your abuser's motivation, but you may be able to make guesses.

The abuser   **Applies to your abuser?**

Was an authoritarian and controlling
  personality   _____

Did not see children as other people but
  as objects to be used   _____

The abuser	Applies to your abuser?
Felt socially and sexually inadequate and insecure with other adults and wanted to abuse children to get sexual gratification without risk of rejection	_____
Was sexually aroused by children	_____
Was sexually, emotionally or physically abused as a child or adult and tried to make him or herself feel more powerful by victimizing someone else	_____
Was another child who was acting out things he or she had experienced or seen	_____
Felt powerless and wanted to exert control over children to feel more powerful	_____
Was full of anger and hate and a desire to hurt and control	_____

2. The Person Overcomes Any Thoughts That Abusing Is Wrong

People who want to abuse know that it is wrong to abuse children. At the very least, they know it is illegal. Before they can put their desires into action, they have to deal with thoughts they may have that abusing is wrong. Abusers may attempt to do this by **justifying** their behavior, **normalizing** their behavior or by **disinhibiting** themselves.

Justifying.   Abusers manage to convince themselves that what they are doing is acceptable by justifying their behavior to themselves in all kinds of ways. They may even justify their behavior to the child they are abusing and convince the child that they have a good reason for abusing. Whatever an abuser thinks or says, there is no good reason for abuse. Abuse does not benefit the child.

Normalizing.   Abusers can create environments for themselves where child sexual abuse is seen as acceptable or normal. The abuser may associate with other people who also abuse children, watch child pornography or read information and listen to comments that appear to support the abuse of children. Some pedophile groups, for example, argue that the age of consent should be abolished on the basis that they are concerned about the sexual rights of children. This can help potential abusers to convince themselves that having sex with children is a way of "sexually liberating" children.

Disinhibiting. Alcohol and drugs lower inhibitions, and people may then do things that they already want to do but might not dare to do when sober. Many abusers drink alcohol before abusing. Drinking alcohol or taking drugs does not cause a person to sexually abuse a child, but if the person already wants to abuse, it may release inhibitions and allow the abuser to act out his or her fantasies. Hypnosis, rituals and dissociation can also put people into altered states and disinhibit them.

EXERCISE 6.4 HOW YOUR ABUSER CAME TO BELIEVE THAT ABUSING WAS OK

Purpose To help you understand how abusers persuade themselves that it is OK to abuse; to help you see that your abuser is responsible for the abuse, not you.

Below is a list of some ways in which abusers overcome their knowledge that abuse is wrong in order to allow themselves to abuse. Check off any that you think might apply to your abuser, and add any others you can think of in the spaces below. *Note:* Again, you are unlikely to know the precise answer to this question, but your abuser may have done or said things that give you a clue.

Justifications

Note: For ease of understanding, survivors are referred to as "she" in the section below. Abusers use the same justifications about boys.

The abuser thinks or says	Applies to your abuser?
I'm just loving her	_____
It's not intercourse, so it's not abuse	_____
It's sex education	_____
She's too young to remember anyway	_____
I'm not hurting her	_____
She enjoys it	_____
The law doesn't understand the special relationship I have with my child	_____
She's my stepdaughter, not my real daughter, so it doesn't count	_____
She is very provocative	_____
I was abused and it didn't harm me	_____

The abuser thinks or says	Applies to your abuser?
She seduced me	_____
She didn't say "No"	_____

Normalize	Applies to your abuser?
Abused in groups with other abusers	_____
Knew other abusers	_____
Read or watched child pornography	_____
Member of pedophile group	_____
Read information from pedophile groups	_____
Had sex with children in other countries where the age of consent is lower or where there is a sex tourism industry	_____

Disinhibit themselves through	Applies to your abuser?
Alcohol	_____
Drugs	_____
Dissociation	_____
Rituals	_____
Other ways of entering altered states	_____

3. The Abuser Gets the Child Alone

For abuse to occur, the abuser must get a child alone or at least away from adults who would be protective. Many children may have come into contact with abusers but have not been abused because the abuser did not get the opportunity. Children who are abused are unlucky enough to have been alone with an abuser or away from people who could protect them.

EXERCISE 6.5
HOW THE ABUSER GOT ACCESS TO YOU

Purpose   To help you understand how your abuser got you on your own or away from other people who might have protected you.

Below is a list of ways in which abusers manage to get children on their own or away from people who would protect them. Check any of the ways that your abuser used. At the end of the list, add any other methods your abuser used.

Applies to your abuser?

Baby-sitting/looking after me　_____

Giving my mom money to go out　_____

Getting friendly with my parent(s)　_____

Taking me on trips　_____

Asking me into his or her house to

- do jobs　_____
- give me candy　_____
- play　_____
- see animals, toys, etc.　_____
- watch TV　_____
- other　_____

Offering me rides　_____

Coming into the bedroom at night　_____

Sharing a bedroom with me　_____

Bathing me　_____

Putting me to bed　_____

Helping me with my homework　_____

Making me share a bed with him or her　_____

Waiting until I got into bed with him or her　_____

Frightening other people into
    not stopping the abuse　_____

Getting me into a shed/garage　_____

Taking me to a lonely place　_____

Having a job that gave access to children
    (such as teacher, social worker, priest)　_____

Doing voluntary work that gave access
    to children (for example, youth club leader,
    scout/guide leader, Sunday school teacher)　_____

Abusing me when other people were around
    without them seeing　_____

Taking opportunities when

- a parent was in the hospital　_____
- a parent was away from home　_____

Other		Applies to your abuser?
_____		_____
_____		_____
_____		_____
_____		_____
_____		_____
_____		_____

The exercise made me see how vulnerable I was. I allowed myself to cry. It made me think about where I stood and what part I played. I saw the situation and it hit me—I had nowhere to go. It happened in the bathtub, the bed, the corner. My dad [the abuser] was all around me and I couldn't get out. I'm beginning to see (not 100 percent) that not all the abuse was my fault. I let them [parents] convince me that it was my fault. —Jean

It was overwhelming to see on paper how easy it is for abusers to abuse and that with the right planning and manipulation children are at risk. —Rebecca

It made me see clearly that it was a plan and not some accident or chance. It helped me to stop making excuses for him [the abuser]. He thought about it and knew what he was doing. —Catherine

4. The Abuser Overcomes the Child's Resistance

The scene for abuse has already been set. The child does not come into the situation until the end. A person who wants to abuse children has persuaded him- or herself that it is OK to abuse and has found a way to get access to a child. The abuser only has to make sure he or she can overcome the child's resistance by manipulating or forcing the child into the abuse. It is easy for abusers to do this.

EXERCISE 6.6
HOW THE ABUSER GOT YOU TO COMPLY

Purpose　To help you understand how your abuser got you to go along with the abuse.

Below is a list of ways in which abusers get children to do what they want. Check off reasons that apply to you and add any others you can think of at the end of the list.

Applies to you?

Adult authority _____

Parental authority _____

Authority of older child _____

Starting the abuse gradually _____

Starting the abuse when you were very young _____

Telling you it was a secret _____

Making you feel sorry for him or her _____

Blaming you for the abuse _____

Threatening you _____

Threatening others if you didn't comply _____

Rewards _____

Treats _____

Confusing you _____

The abuser was bigger than you _____

Violent toward you _____

Violent toward others _____

Giving you alcohol _____

Giving you drugs _____

Pretending it was a game _____

Threatening to abuse your brothers or
    sisters if you objected _____

_____ _____

_____ _____

_____ _____

_____ _____

_____ _____

_____ _____

_____ _____

These are some of the ways that abusers trick, trap and overpower children. You may have noticed that the ways abusers get children to do what they want are the same reasons that we discussed in the last chapter about why children don't stop the abuse or tell anyone. This is not a coincidence; it is in the abuser's interest to make sure that the child does not resist and remains silent about what is happening.

Jean's example

**Jean checked the
  following reasons:**   **and added:**

Adult authority   Said he was doing what fathers do

Parental authority   Said it was all right, he was dad

Starting the abuse gradually   Said he loved me and it was OK

Telling me it was a secret   Said it was loving him

Made me feel sorry for him   He said I was his favorite

Blamed me for what he was doing

Threatened me

Started the abuse when I was
very young

Threats to others if I didn't comply

The abuser was bigger than me

Survivors' comments

I don't think he said anything directly, but indirectly I felt there were threats to others if I didn't comply. Indirectly he let me know it made him happy. I could see he was happy and not yelling at mom or hitting my brother. —*Catherine*

I had feelings of being lost and alone and trapped when I was doing this exercise. Afterward I took the dog for a walk. I needed some air. It helped me think about the exercise again and what I had written. I always believed I could have gotten out of the bathtub or screamed when I was in bed, but fear kept me in there and my parents were the ones who put that fear in me. I am now finding the exercises easier to complete. I am beginning to realize that it was not all my fault. —*Jean*

It made me realize that children cannot be blamed for any kind of abuse because they are innocent. I know I was a child, but I still think I

> could have somehow stopped the abuse. I am annoyed that I let my abusers get away with what they did.   —*Graham*
>
> I feel a little bit that my abuser wasn't consciously aware of the powerful effect he had just by being my dad, an adult, etc. He couldn't appreciate how insignificant I felt in comparison. I can see how I was powerless. He was in total control and therefore totally to blame.   —*Catherine*

Why Did the Abuse Happen to Me?

A child does not cause abuse: an abuser does. For abuse to happen, there must be a person who wants to abuse and who has overcome any misgivings he or she had about doing it. The abuser must then find a place and time when he or she can abuse without being disturbed, and where he or she can frighten or persuade the child into complying. You were unlucky enough to have been in the wrong place at the wrong time.

Coral's Example of Exercises 6.3–6.6

My abuser's motivation:
He wanted power and control.

How my abuser convinced himself it was OK to abuse:
He told himself (and me)

- This is what you want.
- It won't hurt you.
- I'm showing you how much I love you.
- I'm widening your experience and teaching you about life.

How my abuser gained access to me:
He picked out my mother, who was a single parent.
He took a special interest in her children.
He volunteered to watch us while my mother went out.
He took me to his boat.

How my abuser got me to comply:
He told me it was a secret.
He told me that it was a game.
I was too young to understand it was wrong.
It started gradually, so it had been going on a long time before I was aware something was wrong.

I was told by my mother to do what I was told by adults. He threatened me.
He was physically violent to me.

By doing the last four exercises, we hope you are now in a better
position to see that your abuse was caused by your abuser, not you.
However, it is difficult suddenly to give up self-blaming thoughts and
beliefs you have held for many years. The next two exercises help you
continue to challenge your thoughts and beliefs. Remember, it will
probably take longer to get over the feeling that you caused the abuse, but
working on your thoughts is the first step.

EXERCISE 6.7 CHALLENGING THE CHILD'S SELF-BLAME

Go back to Exercise 6.1 and look at all the reasons you have checked in
either column 2 or 3. Write down all these reasons on the left-hand side
of this page under the example below. Now imagine that a child tells
you he or she caused the abuse because of this reason. In the right-hand
column, write down how you would reply in order to make the child
understand that this does not mean he or she is to blame.

Reason   **Your reply**
I cuddled him   Children like to be cuddled. He had no
                               right to abuse you. You are not to blame

_____

_____

_____

_____

_____

_____

_____

_____

_____

_____

Examples

Reason	Your reply
Jean	
I am the middle one	It is not your fault that you are in the middle. It doesn't give anyone the right to abuse you
I'm too loving	So you're too loving, so what? Again, it's no excuse for abuse
I'm lively	You are just enjoying life
Graham	
I am the oldest	That doesn't mean you have to endure abuse from anyone
I am too quiet	They abused your trust and your body—no one has that right
I was put on earth to be abused	No one is put on earth to be abused. It just seems that way when it is happening to you
Rebecca	
I am naughty	A naughty child needs discipline but does not deserve to be abused
Lesley	
I am well developed	He should have controlled himself. You are a child
I enjoyed it	It was a nice feeling, but it was not your fault that he made you feel that way. He was responsible

Survivors' comments

It was hard for me to challenge the child's reasons when I believed these were the reasons it was my fault. When you are a child, you don't want to believe a parent is doing something bad, so you try to find another explanation for being abused. It hurts to realize these reasons aren't true. I've abused myself as well by putting a lot of blame on myself. It is weird to think that none of these reasons make it my fault.   —Jean

I couldn't complete the replies to the child in this exercise for a week after filling in the reasons. I was angry that I was still stuck. Don't be surprised by your reactions. Work through it in your own time. You may have to revisit it several times like I did. —*Rebecca*

I thought of my children and what I would say to them if they said they had been abused. I know now that no matter what, a child is not to blame for the abuse. An adult should always get the blame. In most cases adults know what they are doing. They have to take responsibility for themselves. —*Lesley*

I felt a very powerful difference between my self-blaming and another child self-blaming. It seems bizarre we are so hard on ourselves but so eager to defend other victims of abuse. Until it is pointed out to us, we can't see it. It helped change my very fixed beliefs. —*Catherine*

EXERCISE 6.8 WHAT JUSTIFIES ABUSE?

Purpose To help you understand that your abuser had no right to abuse you, no matter what you were like or what you did or didn't do. Put a checkmark in one of the three columns below.

	Definitely agree	*Maybe agree*	*Do not agree*
A child deserves to be abused if he or she does the following:			
Cuddles people	_____	_____	_____
Sits on someone's knee	_____	_____	_____
Shows his or her underpants	_____	_____	_____
Walks around the house in nightclothes	_____	_____	_____
Walks around the house in underwear	_____	_____	_____
Walks around the house with no clothes on	_____	_____	_____
Gets into bed with a parent	_____	_____	_____
Gets into bed with a relative	_____	_____	_____
Gets into bed with an adult	_____	_____	_____

(continued)

	Definitely agree	Maybe agree	Do not agree
A child deserves to be abused if he or she is the following:			
Pretty/attractive	_____	_____	_____
Ugly	_____	_____	_____
Well developed	_____	_____	_____
Quiet	_____	_____	_____
Lively	_____	_____	_____
Shy	_____	_____	_____
Too loving	_____	_____	_____
Not loving	_____	_____	_____
Naughty	_____	_____	_____
Flirtatious	_____	_____	_____

Nothing **justifies abuse.** Children do not deserve to be abused, no matter what they do or who they are. No matter what you were like, what you said or didn't say, what you did or didn't do, or how you were dressed, this did not cause you to be abused. You were abused because someone who wanted to abuse a child had access to you. Nothing you said or did could have altered the danger you were in. Even if you removed all your clothes and invited the adult to have sex with you, you are not to blame. It is the adult's responsibility not to sexually abuse a child.

Survivors' comments

I was surprised that there were some things I wasn't so sure about. It is helpful to do this with someone trustworthy you can talk to about it. —*Rebecca*

I had a lot of feelings of being a child. My mom said I shouldn't walk around in nightclothes or I'd encourage him. She said, "Don't let him see you in your nightie and he won't do anything." I had to try to remember to do the exercise as a grown-up, but my thoughts kept going back to being a child. As me now, as an adult, I would put them all under "Do not agree with this." —*Jean*

A child never deserves to be abused. —*Catherine*

Though I believe that the abuser is to blame sometimes, even now, I wonder if it was because I was too loving. Fortunately, now I only give it a passing thought when I feel a little low. Having read back through the exercise, I now know that it is not a child's fault, whatever they do. As an adult, you do know whether something is right or wrong in this kind of situation, and for an adult to take advantage of a child is something I will never agree with or understand.   —Anita

In this chapter we have looked at why you might feel you caused the abuse and have tried to help you challenge these reasons. For abuse to occur, a child has to be unlucky enough to be around a person who wants to abuse children and who has convinced him- or herself that it is OK to do so. Then it is very easy for an abuser to get a child to comply. Nothing you did or said was the cause of your being sexually abused; adults are always responsible for sexually abusing a child. It can be hard to suddenly stop blaming yourself, however; the process can take some time. There are also specific reasons why it might be particularly difficult to let go of guilt and self-blame. We explore these reasons in the next chapter.

But I Still Feel Guilty . . .

7

Adult survivors of childhood sexual abuse often struggle to let go of guilty feelings. After working through chapters 5 and 6, you may still feel guilty and believe the abuse was your fault. In this chapter, we look at what can make it particularly difficult for survivors to let go of guilt, and help you explore why you may still feel to blame.

EXERCISE 7.1
WHY DO I STILL FEEL GUILTY?

Purpose   To help you explore why you might find it difficult to let go of guilt.

Below are thoughts and feelings that prevent survivors from letting go of their guilty feelings. Survivors may be aware of some of them. In other cases, their thoughts and feelings may be hidden—survivors may not be consciously aware of them. Read the list of reasons and see if any relate to you.

1) **I got something out of it.**
   You may think you were involved in the abuse or wanted the abuse because you got something out of it, such as attention, money or sexual pleasure.
2) **I had more than one abuser.**
   If you had several abusers, you may believe you attracted the abusers to you.
3) **I was the only person my abuser abused.**
   Thinking you were the only victim of your abuser can make you believe that you in particular were chosen.
4) **I'm frightened of feeling powerless.**
   Believing that you could not stop the abuse can be threatening, because it leaves you feeling that you had no control over what

happened. To avoid feeling powerless in this way, survivors sometimes cling to the idea that they must have caused the abuse or they could have done something to stop it.

5) **I don't want to damage my relationship with the abuser.**
   Survivors sometimes are afraid to believe their abusers are responsible for the abuse, because they do not want to damage or lose their relationship with the abuser. Sometimes it can seem better to believe you were responsible for the abuse in order to maintain your relationship with the abuser.

6) **I'm frightened of my anger.**
   Sometimes survivors are afraid that if they accept that their abusers are responsible for the abuse, they will not be able to contain their anger and will lose control of their behavior.

7) **I know it wasn't my fault, but I still feel guilty.**
   You may know logically or objectively that it could not have been your fault, but you feel guilty anyway.

Write down any of the reasons listed above that apply to you and any others that express why you still feel you are to blame for the abuse:

_____

_____

_____

_____

_____

_____

The reasons above can make it hard for you to accept that you are not to blame for the abuse. The suggestions and exercises in the rest of this chapter can help you explore and challenge each of these reasons.

Examples

I have been abused by so many people that I have always believed I must have wanted it to happen, and that I must have caused so many people to abuse me. After all, I was the one they were all drawn to. —*Sarah*

I know in reality I was not big or powerful enough to stop the abuse, but I still think there must have been something I could have done to stop it. I could and should have stopped it. —*Graham*

1. I Got Something Out of It

> I loved my family despite the abuse, and I knew they wanted me to
> do well in school. I feel guilty because when a teacher began abusing
> me also, I sought him out in the hope of getting good grades to
> please my family and to have a future. —*Thomas*

Survivors often feel guilty because they enjoyed some aspect of the abuse
or felt they got something out of it. Like Thomas, they may have sought
out their abusers because there was something the survivors wanted from
them.

In chapter 5, we saw that abusers have many ways of getting children
to go along with the abuse. They may use threats, but often they offer
children something the children want or need in order to form a
relationship with them and keep them involved in the abuse. For instance,
a child who is neglected at home may be given much-wanted attention,
and this makes the child want to spend time with the abuser. Later this
makes it difficult for the child to tell anyone, because the child believes he
or she encouraged the abuse by seeking out or accepting attention. This is
part of the abuser's plan.

You may have gotten something you wanted from your relationship
with the abuser, such as attention, gifts or cuddling. Receiving these
things or seeking out the abuser for these things does not mean you
wanted to be abused—it means the abuser was offering you things you
wanted so you would be available for abuse.

EXERCISE 7.2
I GOT SOMETHING OUT OF IT

Purpose   To show you that you are not responsible for the abuse if you
got something out of it.

Look at the list below and check any items that applied to you. At
the end, add anything else you got from the abuse:

	Applied to you?
I wanted the attention	_____
I wanted the affection	_____
I liked being special	_____
I liked the presents / money	_____
I enjoyed being taken places by the abuser	_____

(continued)

	Applied to you?
I wanted to keep my relationship with the abuser	_____
I wanted the abuser to protect me from others	_____
I enjoyed the sexual arousal	_____
I wanted to be cuddled	_____
I wanted other things that I got out of it:	_____

Do you know why you wanted these things?

_____

_____

_____

_____

_____

_____

Sarah's example

> I wanted attention and kindness from my abusers.
> I wanted this because I was emotionally neglected by my family and craved attention from anyone—although I usually got the wrong kind of attention. I looked neglected and vulnerable. The abusers were often nice to me at first, so I enjoyed the attention. This made me believe I must have wanted the abuse.

Jonathan's story of why he didn't tell (example from Exercise 5.8) illustrates that knowing you got something from the abusive relationship can make you feel involved in the abuse or responsible for it. Jonathan enjoyed the attention and presents he received from his grandmother, and he responded sexually to her stimulation of his penis. He felt ashamed of his sexual response and this made it much more difficult for him to tell anyone or escape from the abuse.

Many survivors become sexually aroused during their childhood abuse. They may enjoy the physical sensations, or have orgasms, and boys may show visible signs of arousal, such as having an erection or ejaculating. Your sexual organs are designed to respond to sexual stimulation, so responding sexually is a sign that your body is working the way it is supposed to. Boys can have erections as a reflex response to stimulation of their genitals or anal penetration. If you enjoyed the sexual feelings or sought them out, it does not mean you were to blame for the abuse. The abuser used your sexual response to keep you in the abusive relationship. Your sexual feelings may have confused you or made you feel too involved or too ashamed to tell anyone.

As teenagers, survivors may realize more fully that the abuse is not right but continue to submit to it or even seek out the abuser in order to obtain money or other things they want. This can add to their guilt feelings and can be difficult to come to terms with. If this happened to you, remember how the situation developed—the abuser taught you that sexual behavior could be exchanged for other things. This is a dangerous and confusing message for a child or teenager, and your abuser is responsible for teaching you to think and behave in this way. It is not surprising you tried to get what you could from an abusive situation.

The abuse was the responsibility of the abuser, even if you gained something from it. The abuser used your wants and needs to manipulate you and commit a crime against you—you were not to blame.

2. I Had More than One Abuser

When two or more people have abused you, it is easy to think that you were the common factor and that somehow you drew the abusers to you or that something about you caused it to happen.

> I was abused by lots of people because I am not the same as everybody else. Something about me seems to make me get abused. There was some kind of attraction to me.   —*Graham*

It is not unusual for survivors to have been abused by more than one person; more than half of the survivors we have worked with had several abusers. Some survivors have said they felt they had a sign on their foreheads inviting people to abuse them. The next exercise is intended to help survivors who have had more than one abuser reconsider why this might have happened.

EXERCISE 7.3 MULTIPLE ABUSERS

Purpose To help you understand why an abused child may be vulnerable to further abuse by other people.

This exercise is for people who have been abused (as a child or an adult) by more than one person. *Note:* For ease of understanding, the victim is referred to as "she" in the list below.

A. Think about a child who has already been sexually abused. Read all the reasons listed for why she or he may be vulnerable to being abused again by someone else, and check the columns on the right according to whether you think this reason

Would make the child vulnerable to further abuse = **Yes**
Might make the child vulnerable to further abuse = **?**
Would not make the child vulnerable to further abuse = **No**

Makes the child vulnerable to further abuse?	Yes	?	No
She has no adult who will listen to her or believe her	_____	_____	_____
One or both of her parents has already abused her, so she has no one to tell	_____	_____	_____
She has no parents	_____	_____	_____
Her parents are unwilling to protect her	_____	_____	_____
Her parents encourage other people to abuse her	_____	_____	_____
The abuser passes the child or the child's name on to others	_____	_____	_____
Her mother has lots of boyfriends	_____	_____	_____
Her parents take in lodgers so many people have access to her	_____	_____	_____
She couldn't stop the abuse the first time so she doesn't believe she can the next time	_____	_____	_____
She can be blackmailed by someone who knows about the earlier abuse	_____	_____	_____
She blames herself for the first abuse and thinks she deserves any further abuse	_____	_____	_____
It's all she has ever known	_____	_____	_____
She thinks that abuse is all she is good for	_____	_____	_____

Add any other reasons you can think of below:

_____

_____

_____

_____

_____

_____

Survivors who have been abused by more than one person often feel this fact proves something about them caused the abuse to happen. However, they were vulnerable to further abuse because of the situation they were in. In chapter 6, we look at Finkelhor's model, which describes the four steps that must occur before a child is abused. Steps 3 and 4 in this model help us understand why it is common for a child to be abused by more than one person.

Step 3: The abuser gets the child alone.   Children are vulnerable to abuse by several people if they are in a situation that makes it easy for abusers to get access to them. This can happen, for example, when a family takes in lodgers or uses many different baby-sitters or if the child lives away from home in foster care or at boarding school. The danger of further abuse is also increased if children have no one to protect them; for example, when a child has abusive or neglectful parents, no parents, or parents who are regularly absent or ill.

Step 4: The abuser overcomes the child's resistance.   Sexual abuse often has the effect of making children feel powerless and unable to protect themselves. It is easy for another abuser to control a child who has already learned to do as she or he is told and remain silent. Some children feel so helpless and have been abused so often that they begin to accept abuse as inevitable—a "normal" situation that has to be tolerated.

> **Children are only abused by more than one abuser because they are unprotected and several abusers have access to them—not because of who they are.**

Adult survivors may also be vulnerable to further abuse because they feel powerless and unable to defend themselves, they think abuse is "normal," they believe they deserve to be abused, and they may have had little experience of nonabusive relationships.

  B. Think about your own situation and write down why you think you were abused by more than one person. You may want to write an account of your experience or write a list of reasons. Use the list above to give you some ideas.

> When I was doing this exercise, it helped me to think of a child I know being in the same situation that I was in and to imagine what she felt.   —*Sarah*

Why I Was Abused by More Than One Person

Examples

Pauline

I thought it was my fault that so many people abused me because they sensed that I would let them. Doing this exercise made me realize I couldn't have done anything at the time. I can see and understand how things were for me then. I was too frightened to say "No," and it felt like everybody knew that I would let them do whatever they wanted. They knew I was vulnerable, and they could get away with it because I didn't dare say anything to anybody. I was afraid for my life. I'd been abused by so many people that I thought everyone must have known what was happening. It felt like I deserved to be abused, and I thought they might love me if I let them do it.

Now I know that I was abused by so many people because there were so many abusers around me and each one of the pathetic beings had access to *ME.*

Sarah

I was exposed to abuse from an early age, so I never learned I had a right to say "No." It was all I ever knew.

My parents took in boarders and several of them abused me. I recently discovered that one of the boarders had been accused of molesting little girls.

My name was passed from one abuser to another.

Sarah felt distressed and angry after she had done the exercise. This is how she coped with her feelings.

I cried a lot. I dealt with my anger by punching my punching bag. Then I found it really helped to write letters (for myself—not to send) to all my abusers telling them how I felt and how pathetic they were.

Although the exercise brought up strong feelings, Sarah found it was useful.

I felt relief when I did this exercise because I began to see that I did not want the abuse or cause it. I also felt angry that the abusers were so weak that they had to prey on a helpless, vulnerable child. It feels like the beginning of letting go of the guilt and responsibility.

3. I Was the Only Person My Abuser Abused

Sometimes abusers do just abuse one child in a family. They often find ways of isolating the child from the rest of the family by making him or her feel different or special; for example, in Jonathan's situation, his grandmother singled him out for special attention. Abusers may tell their victims they chose them because they were special, because they loved them, because they were bad and they were punishing them, or for any of the other reasons described in chapter 6. They find ways of making their victims feel responsible for the abuse in order to manipulate them into keeping silent. Even if you were the only victim, your abuser is still responsible for the abuse.

However, most abusers do not usually select one "special" child to abuse and then stop. They go on abusing children whenever they get the opportunity or can create one. Abusers often have many victims, who may be from inside or outside the family. Sisters and brothers may each spend years believing they are the only one in the family who has been abused. If one person has been keeping the abuse secret, other people have probably been doing the same. You may think you were the only child chosen by your abuser, when in reality he or she abused other children also. As adults, survivors frequently discover that family members or other people have been abused by the same person they were.

4. I'm Frightened of Feeling Powerless

Doing the exercises in chapter 5 made me see that my abusers were at least twice as big as me and over twenty years older. I felt overwhelmed, small and insignificant. I feel angry with the abusers because I was so little and weak and unable to protect myself. I got angry about the power imbalance between me and them. Although it helped me see how I couldn't stop the abuse, it left me feeling powerless and vulnerable.   —Rebecca

When you believe you are to blame for the abuse, you can at least feel you had some control over what was happening. Realizing you did not cause the abuse and could not stop it can relieve feelings of guilt, but it can also be frightening to realize you had no control over the situation and were so powerless. Feeling powerless, or the fear of being powerless, can make it hard to let go of feelings of self-blame.

I coped with feeling so powerless and vulnerable by talking it through
with someone and reminding myself that things are different now, and
I am no longer that child. —Rebecca

You *were* powerless and vulnerable as a child, but you are an adult now.
The next two exercises are designed to help you become more aware of
the greater strength and power you have now.

Your Physical Size and Power Now

Exercise 5.4 demonstrated that your abuser was probably bigger and
stronger than you were when the abuse began, to help establish the fact
that you could not have stopped the abuser physically. In the next
exercise, you are asked to compare your size now to your abuser's current
size. It is important that you draw your abuser at the size he or she is now,
not how big you *feel* he or she is. Distance yourself from your feelings
about the abuser as best you can and think objectively about what his or
her actual size is now.

EXERCISE 7.5 PHYSICAL SIZE NOW

Purpose To help you feel less powerless in relation to your abuser by
looking at the difference in physical size between you and your abuser
now.

Draw a picture of yourself and your abuser as you both are now.
(Drawing stick figures is fine.)

Me as I am now   My abuser now

There is probably much less difference in size between you and the abuser now compared to when the abuse began. Some of you will now be bigger than your abuser.

Write down any thoughts and feelings that came up for you when you were doing this exercise:

_____

_____

_____

_____

_____

_____

_____

_____

_____

I'm the same size as my mother now, and I realize it can never happen again.   —Graham

You may feel vulnerable because your abuser is still bigger than you are or because it still feels as though the abuser has all the power. The next exercise helps you look at the difference between the power you had at the time of the abuse and the power you have now. It is useful to do this exercise even if your abuse is ongoing.

EXERCISE 7.6   POWER NOW

Purpose   To help you see the abuser no longer has all the power by looking at the power you have now.

In Exercise 5.3, you looked at the kinds of power your abuser had over you as a child. You do have more power now than you did then, though you may not be aware of it. In this exercise, you will be looking at the kinds of power you have now. Below we list some of the reasons children are powerless *at the time of the abuse* and also why adult survivors *do* have more power now. Read the list and check any statements that apply to you. Add any other reasons you can think of.

	Applies to you?		**Applies to you?**
During the abuse you were		**Now you are**	
A child or teenager	_____	An adult	_____
Physically small	_____	Physically larger	_____
Trapped by the abuser	_____	Not trapped by the abuser	_____
Powerless	_____	Working on taking control	_____
Silenced by the secret	_____	Telling or thinking of telling someone	_____
Dependent on the abuser	_____	Not dependent on the abuser	_____
During the abuse you had		**Now you have**	
No knowledge of abuse	_____	Information and knowledge	_____
No one around who would have believed you	_____	People around who know and believe about child abuse	_____
No one to tell	_____	People you could tell	_____
During the abuse		**Now**	
The abuser was strong	_____	The abuser is older, weaker or dead	_____
You were confused about what was happening	_____	You know it was abuse and it was illegal	_____
You blamed yourself	_____	You know the abuser was responsible	_____

Write down any sources of power you have now that you did not have as a child. (Use the list above to help you.)

_____

_____

_____

_____

_____

_____

The exercise above may have increased your awareness of the power you have now. By working through this book you are gradually building your own power and strength.

> I realized I can get out of my abuser's clutches—it is coming. I am getting there. I am stronger now.   —*Jean*

It's a Crime

> As a child I was powerless, and I was blackmailed not to tell anyone. Now that I've had therapy, I have been confident enough to tell the police and the courts. This helped me get my power back.   —*Pauline*

Having any form of sexual contact with a child is a *crime* even if the child "agreed" to it. One form of power you have now is the knowledge that the abuser committed a crime and that you have the power to report the abuser to the police. We are not suggesting that you actually go to the police. That is a step to consider carefully, and you need to be prepared for what might happen if you decide to go that route. There are no time limits on prosecution for major crimes such as child abuse, but there is rarely enough evidence to successfully prosecute for abuse that happened years ago. Most important is that *you* are aware that the abuser committed an illegal act, and that *you* know you have the power to inform the police and that they would take your report seriously.

Note: If you do decide to report your abuser to the police, be sure to talk it through with someone first, so you are fully aware of the consequences and how you may be affected. Contact your local social-services office or one of the helplines in the resources section at the end of the book and talk it over with a knowledgeable person.

As a child, you were under the power of your abuser. You may have learned to initiate the abuse or seek out the abuser so you could at least feel you had some control over what was happening. This may have helped you survive the abuse rather than feel totally powerless because of it.

As an adult, you may still feel you are to blame for the abuse because you believe you should have been able to stop it or because you sought out the abuser. It may be difficult to give up feeling responsible for the abuse because you are afraid that then you will feel powerless. To overcome this fear, first you need to accept the fact that you were powerless as a child and therefore not responsible for the abuse—and that you are *not* powerless now. Your power grows as you release the guilt that is holding you back and as you break free from the effects of the abuse.

You may still have symptoms that make you feel out of control, such as panic attacks and sleep problems, and you may be using coping strategies such as obsessive-compulsive behaviors, being aggressive and controlling your body size and eating to make you feel more in control of your life. If you feel out of control or experience any of these problems, remind yourself that you have greater strength and power now than you did as a child. Learning to take control of your symptoms will help you feel more powerful and more in control. It may also enable you to stop feeling guilty. Some of the problems can be difficult to overcome by yourself, and you may need to seek professional help.

5. I Don't Want to Damage My Relationship with the Abuser

Often survivors are afraid of placing responsibility for the abuse with their abusers because they do not want to damage their relationship with the abuser or change their view of him or her. Children are dependent on families or caregivers for their emotional and physical well-being and usually want to keep their relationships intact, even if these people are abusing them. Adult survivors may feel loyal to their abusers, especially if they are family members. Survivors may feel they would be betraying their family members if they were to blame them for the abuse. However, it is abusers who betray the trust of children in their care, and they are responsible for their actions.

All children want to feel loved by their parents and other people close to them. Being abused by a parent or someone you love can create a huge inner conflict. It is hard to believe that someone who loves you could deliberately harm you. Sometimes children find it easier to believe the abuse was their fault rather than the fact that the abuser was willing to harm them for his or her own desires. Survivors may believe that they caused the abuser to abuse them, and they sometimes say things such as, "It was my fault because I was naughty," or "He only did it because I wanted him to." By taking responsibility for the abuse, the survivor can continue to see the abuser as a loving, caring person.

Annabelle loved her father and found it hard to accept that he had abused her. As a child, she had separated him in her mind into two people—a loving father and the "bye-bye man" who abused her in the night:

It would be much easier to come to terms with having been abused if your abuser were an ugly stranger. When that person is your father, someone you would expect to love and protect you, then it becomes more complicated. To see your father as someone who is capable of terrifying his own child into participating in sexual activities is so devastatingly threatening that you prefer to doubt your own experience and sanity. You need a father who is kind and protective, not the "bye-bye man" who lurks in the shadows of your bedroom. You become very protective toward your abuser and start to idealize him. Whatever he says or does is always right. You feel special when you are with him and want that to continue. You seek out sexual activity and you may actually enjoy what is happening and experience orgasms. You cannot let your mother know, because you have been a willing part of it. She would accuse you of being bad and a slut and she would be right.   *—Annabelle*

Annabelle could not see her father as responsible for the abuse because she wanted to retain her memories of a loving relationship with him. She saw her father as someone who never did anything wrong. Instead, she blamed herself for seeking him out for attention and sexual activity.

Think about the following questions:

- Were you emotionally or physically dependent on your abuser?
- Was the relationship with the abuser important to you?
- Do you love your abuser?

If you answered "Yes" to any of these questions and you are still blaming yourself for the abuse, you may be trying to protect your abuser or your relationship with your abuser. Try to accept that you may have tolerated the sexual acts or sought out the abuser because you wanted to keep your relationship with the abuser or your view of the abuser as a caring person. The sexual activity was the responsibility of the abuser— you were not to blame. You do not have to continue holding yourself responsible for the abuse in order to maintain your relationship with the abuser. It is possible to continue loving someone as well as giving him or her the responsibility for the abuse.

6. I'm Frightened of My Anger

Once you begin to realize that you are not to blame for the abuse, you may start to feel angry. Some survivors describe feelings of rage and hatred so powerful that they fear they will not be able to contain them. They may be afraid that they will act inappropriately or become aggressive or violent. Survivors describe urges to confront their abusers, attack them or even kill them. Angry feelings may also be directed at other people, such as the nonabusing parent who failed to protect, or at people who do not understand. Some survivors have learned to turn their anger on themselves and may fear they will harm themselves.

Angry feelings can be overwhelming, and it is no wonder that some survivors retreat into blaming themselves for the abuse. Blaming yourself can be easier and more comfortable than dealing with feelings of murderous rage. Survivors have usually been unable to express their anger directly during their childhood, so they have had to find other ways of dealing with it. Blaming yourself can be seen as a coping strategy—a way of containing your anger and keeping yourself and other people safe. It is not always easy to know whether you are blaming yourself as a way of containing your anger. Many of these processes happen outside our conscious awareness. Try to answer the questions below without censoring your thoughts and feelings.

- If you stop blaming yourself for the abuse, who or what might you feel angry about?
- What do you fear you might do or what might happen if you experienced that anger?

Here are a few suggestions:

- Accept that your guilt may be a way of containing your anger. When you feel confident about dealing with your anger safely, you will be in a better position to let go of the guilt.
- Work on being assertive and acknowledging and dealing with angry feelings in everyday situations as they arise, rather than bottling your anger.
- Remember that feelings of anger and thoughts of revenge are common reactions to trauma. Many people experience these thoughts and feelings but do not act on them.
- If you are tempted to act violently, think about the consequences. Violence can feel like a solution but actually creates more problems.
- If you think you are in serious danger of harming someone else or yourself, seek professional help.
- Anger can be expressed safely and nonviolently. Explore ways of dealing with your anger by reading a book about it, talking to other

people about how they cope or working with a therapist. The next exercise will help you find ways of coping with anger.

EXERCISE 7.7 SAFE WAYS OF EXPRESSING ANGER

Purpose To help you find ways of expressing anger safely and nonviolently.

Write a list below of all the ways you could express anger safely, without harming yourself or others. It may help to ask other people how they cope with anger.

_____

_____

_____

_____

_____

_____

_____

_____

Example

This is a list produced by one survivors' group with which we work:

Scream	Phone someone
Write down how I feel	Paint or draw
Talk to a chair	Talk to a therapist
Write a letter	Punch my pillow or punching bag
Talk into a tape	Hit a cushion/hit the bed
Use a stress doll	Do physical exercise

7.1 Know It Wasn't My Fault, but I Still Feel Guilty

You may now understand that you couldn't stop the abuse or tell anyone, and that it was *not* your fault that you were abused or that the abuse continued over months or years. However, you may still *feel* it was your fault. It is easier to change the way you think than to change the way you feel. It can take time for changes in your feelings to catch up with changes in the way you think. Whenever you feel guilty, look over the last two chapters again. Better yet—repeat the exercises. Over time, this activity will help your feelings change as well as your beliefs, so you no longer *feel* to blame or *feel* guilty. Try the next exercise.

EXERCISE 7.8 ABUSERS ARE ALWAYS RESPONSIBLE FOR ABUSE

Purpose   To remind yourself every day that you are not responsible for the abuse.

It takes time to change feelings you have had for many years, but you can help promote this change by regularly challenging old beliefs. Write the following words on a piece of paper and put the paper somewhere where you will see the words every day or say them to yourself every morning.

It doesn't matter what a child does. Sexual abuse only occurs when an abuser has access to a child. Abusers are always responsible for abuse.

It doesn't matter what I did. I was sexually abused because an abuser had access to me.

Guilt, Shame and Blame

Why not try Exercises 5.1 and 5.2 again to see if anything has changed in your beliefs about who is responsible for sexual abuse? Even a small change means you are beginning to challenge the beliefs you have held for so long. Don't worry if you have completed the exercises in this chapter and still think the abuse was your fault. The chapter on abusers will help you continue to work on who is responsible for the abuse and on regaining your power in relation to the abuser. You may also benefit from talking through your feelings with a friend or a support person or by contacting a telephone helpline. Return to this chapter later and try the exercises again.

The three chapters in this section have focused on challenging your beliefs that you were to blame for the abuse and on shifting the responsibility for the abuse to the abuser where it belongs. The next section helps you explore and process your feelings toward the people who were around at the time of the abuse—the abuser, your mother or other nonabusive caregiver, and toward yourself as a child.

PART 3

Feelings about Yourself and Others

This section helps you focus on your relationship with, and feelings about, significant figures in your childhood:

- Your abuser (chapter 8)
- Your mother or main nonabusing caregiver (chapter 9)
- Yourself as a child (chapter 10)

8

Abusers

The exercises in this chapter are intended to help you better understand your feelings toward your abuser and to begin to feel empowered in relation to your abuser. Your abuser may have been a man or a woman, a family member, a neighbor, someone you knew because of their job (for example, a priest, social worker or teacher), a friend of the family or a stranger. Your abuser may have been much older than you or a similar age. You may have regular contact with your abuser, you may have no idea where he or she is now, or your abuser may be dead. You may have had one abuser, many different abusers or have been abused by a group. The abuse may be still happening. Whatever the situation was then, and whatever the circumstances are now, these exercises are for you.

As you work on the exercises, be prepared for strong feelings to appear, and make sure you know how to cope if this happens. Many adult survivors of childhood sexual abuse still feel powerless in relation to their abuser and may experience feelings of fear or terror when they begin to think about him or her. Therefore think carefully about when and where it feels safe to do these exercises. Go back to chapters 1 and 3 and decide whom you can contact and what coping strategies you will use if needed.

Approach these exercises with special care if you have a problem with flashbacks or if you see or hear your abuser when he or she is not there. The exercises could trigger such experiences, so first make sure you have worked through the exercises in chapter 4 about dealing with flashbacks and hallucinations. Be sure you feel confident about handling your reactions. Try to keep in mind that you are an adult now and have more power than you did as a child.

If you have had more than one abuser, photocopy the exercises first and repeat the exercises for each abuser. It may help to start with the abuser you feel least fearful of.

Feelings toward Your Abuser

The first two exercises provide different ways to help you explore your feelings toward your abuser. You may want to work through one or both exercises.

EXERCISE 8.1   TALKING TO A CHAIR

Purpose   To help you express your feelings to your abuser and to feel more empowered.

Sit on a chair and pick another chair to represent your abuser. Place this chair opposite you at whatever feels the most comfortable distance. Imagine this chair is your abuser. You are able to talk to your abuser but he or she is not able to speak to you.

Talk to your abuser and tell him or her whatever you want to. Start by telling your abuser what he or she has done to you and how it has affected your life. Be aware of how you are feeling. You may experience one type of emotion most strongly—anger, love, fear, hate, distress, pity, distaste—or mixed emotions. Accept whatever feelings come up and express these feelings to your abuser.

Make a note below of any feelings that appeared when you were talking to your abuser.

_____

_____

_____

_____

_____

_____

_____

_____

Example
One support group's feelings toward their abusers:

Hate	Nothing
Warmth	Anger
Fear	Indifference
Disappointment	Sorry for him

Despise him
Murderous
Rage
Revulsion
Loathing
Ashamed of her
Disgust

Compassion
Pity
Protective
Love
Terror
Forgiving

Survivors' comments

I felt anger, repugnance, fear, pity, revenge and power while I did this exercise. I let myself feel like this. It helped me get it off my chest. Don't hold anything back. You can censor it or discard it later.
—*Maya*

Even though I am post-therapy, this exercise was useful because it let me know where my feelings were at the moment. Even though I have worked through the anger stage of my recovery, I realized I still have a problem with feeling responsible for my abuser's happiness. —*Catherine*

Fear was the most powerful feeling I got, but the more I talked, the more I realized there is no way he can hurt me anymore. I am an adult now, not a child. I can show him that he does not frighten me anymore. —*Lesley*

There is no right or wrong way to feel about your abuser. Allow whatever feelings you have to surface; you may be surprised by what you discover. Survivors often have mixed feelings about their abusers. They may have feelings of hatred toward and also feelings of love for or a desire to protect the abuser, especially if the abuser is someone close, such as a family member. Other people might try to tell you how they think you should feel. You might also tell yourself how you ought to feel rather than simply accepting how you *do* feel. It can be difficult to admit to yourself or to other people that you love someone who has done awful things to you. It can also be difficult to admit to feelings of anger or hatred toward your abuser, particularly if he or she is a close family member. However, it is more helpful to understand how you are actually feeling rather than try to force yourself to feel a certain way. Some survivors, particularly survivors with strong religious beliefs, feel they should forgive their abuser. They try to bury their feelings of anger in order to do this. This can be an added burden and delay the healing process. Feelings of forgiveness may come in time for some survivors, but it is not a feeling that can be rushed or forced, nor is it a feeling that you can simply decide to have.

EXERCISE 8.2   LETTER TO THE ABUSER

Purpose   To explore and express your feelings to your abuser and to feel empowered.

Write a letter to your abuser using the space below. Allow plenty of time for this exercise. This letter is *not* meant to be sent; it isn't a letter for the abuser but a way of working on your own feelings. Write whatever comes into your head. You may want to describe the things the abuser did to you, and how it made you feel at the time. You may want to tell him or her how the abuse affected your life as you got older and how you feel about him or her now. You don't have to begin the letter with "Dear." Some survivors do not want to address their abusers in this way. Start the letter in whatever way feels comfortable.

DO NOT SEND THIS LETTER to your abuser. Doing these exercises can sometimes make survivors start to feel strong and powerful, and it can be tempting to act on these feelings. However, confronting your abuser by letter or in person can have consequences that can be extremely difficult to handle and can leave you feeling disempowered. Remember, this exercise is designed to help you work on your own feelings. *It is for you alone;* it isn't about trying to communicate with your abuser or getting a response from him or her.

Examples

Lesley's letter
Lesley was sexually abused by her brother.

> You bastard, I wish I had a gun. I want to kill you for what you did to me. Try putting your dick in my mouth now and you won't have one left. You got a lot out of hurting someone smaller than you, but now I am an adult and I can stand up for myself. You will never hurt me again. You took my childhood away from me and made me feel things a child should never feel. If I hear that you have hurt anybody else the way you hurt me I will make your life a mess just like you have made mine.

Nina's letter
Nina was sexually abused by the housemother of a children's home.

> You creep. I don't know what else to class you as. You are not an animal—they have feelings, you don't. I want to tell you how you made me feel when you did those awful things to me. I felt like a robot sometimes. You would never let me show any emotion. You wanted to control me, even my thoughts. You never considered how you made me feel. Do you remember how you would touch me and put things in me? You knew I didn't like it, you knew I was very frightened, but you continued just to please yourself. You would use your cigarette to burn me and know that it hurt, but you never stopped. How do you think I felt? I felt used and dirty. I didn't have a mind of my own. You would say things to make me feel bad about myself. You wanted to make me feel worthless, that I was a nobody, and you succeeded. I didn't like myself. I felt I shouldn't breathe the same air as other people. You made me feel so useless, not worthy to be a human. I would let people do what they wanted and never speak up for myself. You made me feel that and I hate and detest you for it.
>
> I am writing this letter to you but it isn't for your benefit. This is so I can let you know what kind of a creep you are. Also to let you know that you haven't destroyed me. In fact, I am a stronger person. I survived.

I will never forgive you for what you did. Not just me but the other kids as well. It makes me feel cleaner, getting you out of my system. I will keep fighting until I get you out of my system forever. Soon you will be nothing. I'll be back because I haven't finished with you yet.

Maya's letter

Maya was abused by her mother, other family members and also by a storekeeper.

To the sad, sick storekeeper who abused me:

I guess you felt powerful when you forced your horrible tongue into my mouth until I couldn't breathe. I should have bitten it off. Even after all this time I am afraid of having dental treatment because it reminds me of what you did. And groping me with your disgusting dirty hands. How dare you defile me with your filth?

This letter is to give you back all the bad feelings, the guilt, shame and fear that isn't mine. I now absolve myself of these things and place them firmly back where they belong—with you. I despise you. —*Maya*

Graham's letter

Graham was sexually abused by his mother.

Mother,

For as long as I remember I have wanted to say exactly what I thought of you. Obviously I waited too long because now you are dead and I didn't get the chance to ask you, "Why me?" I always knew you didn't like me from a very early age, even to the point of hating me. I don't know what I did to deserve the treatment I got, but I know you won't rest in peace, you don't deserve to. The hatred and anger I have for you is overwhelming. I am grateful, however, that you are not here to abuse my children, and to be perfectly honest, I am glad they never knew you.

I often ask why I had to have you for my mother. Why didn't you have me adopted? I probably would have had a better life and not been beaten or treated like a dog, but you couldn't even do that for me. I am now an adult, but you left me scarred. Instead of beating me, you should have loved me, but your only priority was your next bottle of beer. I should have been able to come to you for help and advice and not a kick in the teeth.

I want to forget you, but the effect you had on my life has been too great. I know I put too much energy into hating you, but you are not going to ruin my marriage or my children because I won't let you. I won't even visit your grave because you don't deserve my tears. I won't cry for you and I won't let you ruin the rest of my life. I want to live my life for me.

Survivors' comments

It gave me confidence to express myself without apologizing. I felt some fear while I was completing the exercise, but I kept writing and felt stronger afterward. I felt satisfied with the results. Giving the feelings back felt good. Go for it! Tell yourself you can do it.   —*Maya*

This was a powerful exercise—once I started writing, the thoughts seemed to flow. It would be easy to blank out the memories for the sake of other members of the family. But it is important for me to have a reminder of the extent of the damage and how it affected my life. I tend to try and please others. This letter helped me put my thoughts in order and feel that I am still managing to put myself first and to feel empowered against my abuser. I feel much more confident writing my thoughts rather than talking aloud. Seeing my thoughts written down makes them much more real than just words floating in the air. Having written a letter, it could be tempting to mail it. Don't do it—you'd regret it later.   —*Catherine*

Say what you really feel. Don't hold anything back. It's important!
—*Rebecca*

Standing Up to Your Abuser in Your Imagination

The exercises in the next section are intended to help you overcome feelings of fear about your abuser and to feel more empowered. They also help to reinforce the knowledge that what happened to you was not right and that you were not to blame for being abused. Before you start, keep in mind that these exercises are to be done on paper or in your imagination, *not in person with your abuser.*

This section is divided into four steps:

- What you would like to say to your abuser.
- How abusers usually react to confrontations and how *your* abuser might react.
- How to respond assertively to your abuser.
- An imaginary confrontation with your abuser.

Confronting your abuser *in your thoughts* can be a powerful and liberating experience for survivors. Confronting your abuser in person is a very different matter and can be dangerous to you, both physically and psychologically. These exercises are *not* intended to help you confront your abuser in person but to help you understand more about your own thoughts and feelings about the abuse and the abuser. *Do not use the exercises below face-to-face with your abuser.*

1. What Do You Want to Say?

Think about what you would like to say to your abuser if you had the opportunity and if you felt strong and powerful enough to say anything you wanted to. Think about what you said in Exercise 8.1 and what you wrote in Exercise 8.2. Do you want to express how you feel about the abuse or about your abuser? Do you want to tell the abuser how he or she has damaged your life?

EXERCISE 8.3   WHAT DO YOU WANT TO SAY?

Purpose   To think clearly about what you would like to say to your abuser as a first step toward confronting your abuser in your imagination.

Write down below anything you would like to say to your abuser as a series of brief statements.

What I want to say to my abuser.
For example, "You masturbated in front of me when I was a child and I am very angry with you." "I have an eating problem now because you raped me as a child."

_____

_____

_____

_____

_____

_____

_____

_____

Catherine's example

> You hit my brother. I heard you. You made me live in fear. I heard mom
> crying at night and you shouting at her. You touched me between my
> legs while smiling at me and telling me it was nice. Because of you I
> became anorexic, bulimic and regularly slashed my arms. The effects of
> your abuse lasted twenty years—think about that. I was three years
> old and had done nothing to deserve any of this.

2. Abusers' Reactions

When abusers are confronted about the abuse in person, they rarely admit
to what they did. They usually deny the abuse happened or **minimize**
what really happened by pretending it wasn't sexual abuse but something
innocent or loving. Some abusers **blame** the survivor for what happened,
often by suggesting the survivor wanted the abuse or caused it in some
way—these may be the same things the abuser said to the survivor as a
child. Some abusers threaten the survivor for talking about the abuse and
again, this may be a familiar pattern from childhood.

Abusers might also try to make the survivor feel sorry for him or her
by making excuses or talking about their own problems—they may try to
guilt-trip the survivor into remaining silent. Abusers might try to **confuse**
the survivor or divert the conversation by throwing in red herrings
(diversions that are meant to put the conversation offtrack); for example,
by challenging details of what has been said or expecting the survivor to
prove what he or she has said. Examples of each of these types of
reactions follow:

Denying	I don't know what you're talking about.
Minimizing	I was only tickling you.
Blaming	You got into bed with me.
Threatening	No one will talk to you again.
Excusing	I was under a lot of stress at the time.
Guilt-tripping	You know my health isn't good. Why are you being so mean to me?
Red herrings	You say I did these things in my car. Then tell me what kind of car it was!

By understanding more about the ways abusers try to deny or
minimize the abuse, and blame, threaten or confuse their victims, and by
naming these reactions, you are better able to step back and see your
abuser's responsibility for the abuse more clearly.

EXERCISE 8.4   MY ABUSER'S REACTIONS

Purpose   To anticipate how your abuser might react if you challenged him or her as a second step toward confronting your abuser in your imagination.

Think about how your own abuser might react if you said the things you wrote down in Exercise 8.3, and write down these reactions below as short statements.

Abuser's reactions

For example, "You kept taking your clothes off in front of me."

_____

_____

_____

_____

_____

_____

3. Responding Assertively to Your Abuser

By learning how to challenge abusers' reactions by responding assertively (in the exercise, not in person), you can begin to feel more in control and more powerful compared to your abuser.

Below are some examples of abusers' reactions. In the right-hand column are examples of how to respond assertively to each type of reaction.

Abusers' reactions	Assertive response
Denying	
I don't know what you're talking about.	Yes, you do, you made me touch your penis.
You're crazy/a liar.	No, I am not crazy/a liar. You masturbated on me.
I did no such thing.	Yes, you did. You fondled my breasts.
Minimizing	
I only tickled you.	You not only tickled me, you put your fingers in my vagina.
I was only cuddling you and being affectionate.	You were not being affectionate, you anally raped me.

Abusers' reactions	Assertive response
Blaming	
You got into bed with me.	Yes, I did, but I was a child. You raped me, and that is your responsibility.
You had an erection. You wanted it.	Yes, I had an erection. That is a natural response to being masturbated, but you were abusing me and you are responsible.
Threatening	
No one will talk to you again.	I am not to blame, you are responsible. You forced me to perform oral sex.
I'll tell your partner what you did.	You are responsible for the abuse. I am not to blame.
Excusing	
I was under a lot of stress at the time.	You may have been under a lot of stress, but that does not excuse the fact that you were an adult and you masturbated in front of me.
Guilt-tripping	
You know I'm not in good health. Why are you being so nasty to me?	I am not being nasty, I am stating the truth. You anally raped me when I was a child, and you are responsible for what you did.
I've had a lot of experiences in my life, too, but I don't make a big deal about it.	You may have had bad experiences, but that does not give you the right to masturbate me. I have every right to make a "big deal" about what you did to me.
Red herrings	
You say I did these things in my car. Then tell me what kind of car it was!	I am not here to talk about cars. You raped me and you are responsible.

How to Respond Assertively

- Keep replies short and simple.
- Deny anything that is untrue in what the abuser has said.
- State clearly what is true.
- Be specific about what the abuser actually did; for example, "You put your finger in my bottom," rather than, "You sexually abused me."
- Do not get sidetracked by irrelevant details—say they are irrelevant.

Remember: You are not trying to prove what happened but to make a clear statement about what you know happened and to express your feelings. Whatever the circumstances, a child is never to blame for being sexually abused. You are the victim of a crime, and the abuser could still be prosecuted for that crime, no matter how long ago it happened.

EXERCISE 8.5   RESPONDING ASSERTIVELY TO YOUR ABUSER IN IMAGINATION

Purpose   To think of assertive responses to your abuser's imaginary reactions as a way of feeling more empowered and as a third step in confronting your abuser in imagination.

1) Below are more examples of ways in which abusers might react if challenged about what they did. Write an assertive response to each of these reactions in the right-hand column. Keep replies simple: Deny what isn't true and state what is true. Look back at the examples for ideas about how to reply.

Abuser's reactions	Assertive response
You are sick in the head.	_____
I was only loving you.	_____
I was teaching you the facts of life.	_____
You enjoyed it.	_____
You didn't say "No."	_____
You'd better be careful what you say, or else.	_____
I've had a hard life.	_____
I've already had one heart attack—you're going to give me another one.	_____
We weren't living in that house when you were seven.	_____

2) Write down your abuser's reactions (from Exercise 8.4) in the left-hand column, and for each of your abuser's reactions write an assertive response. Be as specific as possible in saying what the abuser did to you; for example, "You made me suck your penis," rather than, "You sexually abused me." Don't be sidetracked by irrelevant details (red herrings); for example, arguments about when certain things happened in your childhood.

Abuser's reactions	Assertive response
————————	————————
————————	————————
————————	————————
————————	————————
————————	————————
————————	————————
————————	————————
————————	————————
————————	————————
————————	————————
————————	————————

Examples

Abuser's reactions	Assertive response

Catherine's example

| I loved you. | That is irrelevant. |
| You probably would have had problems anyway. | No. Your abuse caused these problems. |

Anthony's example

I don't know what you're talking about.	Yes you do, and you can't deny it. You touched me by playing with my penis.
You are a liar.	There is only one liar here and it isn't me.
You enjoyed it as much as I did.	No, I did not enjoy it. If I reacted to your touching my penis or other parts of my body it is because that is a normal reaction.

(continued)

Abuser's reactions	**Assertive response**
You kept taking your clothes off in front of me.	That is normal. When you are a child you take your clothes off in front of someone when you are getting ready for bed or getting ready to take a bath. I was not asking to be abused, but you abused me.

Lesley's example	
You didn't look like a child.	I was well developed but I was still a child.
You deserved what you got.	Nobody deserves to be abused and frightened like I was.

> *Survivor's comment*
>
> Because it was so concise, this was an empowering exercise. I could put the abuser back where he belonged. It also helped confirm in my mind that the abuse did happen. —*Catherine*

4. Imaginary Confrontation

Now you can try to put the whole thing together with an imaginary confrontation with your abuser. *This is an exercise only and is **not** to be done face to face with your abuser.* Remember:

- State what is true and say what isn't true.
- Don't be drawn into arguments over irrelevant details.
- Keep repeating what you know is true, whatever the abuser's reaction. This is the "broken record" technique—you keep saying the same thing again and again like an old record when the needle is stuck in one place.

Below we describe three ways in which you can do this. Choose one method that suits you best, or try them all.

EXERCISE 8.5   ROLE-PLAY CONFRONTATION

Purpose   To role-play a confrontation with your abuser as a way of feeling more empowered in relation to him or her and of challenging negative reactions to yourself.

Chair role-play

- Get two chairs, one to represent you and one to represent your abuser, as you did in Exercise 8.1. Place them a comfortable distance apart.
- Sit in the chair that represents you and speak to your abuser. Say the things you would like to say if you could—the things you have written down in Exercise 8.3.
- Swap chairs and talk back to yourself as if you are your abuser, using your abuser's reactions that you wrote down in Exercise 8.4.
- Return to your own chair and reply to your abuser as yourself, using the responses from Exercise 8.5.
- Continue swapping chairs and confronting your abuser until you feel ready to stop.

Remember, you are in charge of this conversation and can stop it whenever you want to.

Role-play with a friend

Ask a trusted person if he or she will help you role-play a confrontation with your abuser. Talk to your friend about the work you have been doing in this chapter or ask him or her to read this chapter. Make sure your friend understands the kind of things you want to say to your abuser, the range of ways in which the abuser might react, and how to respond assertively to these reactions.

Now role-play the confrontation with your friend. If your friend can make good, assertive responses, it may help to start by playing the abuser and let your friend play you. Once you have done this, swap roles so your friend plays the abuser and you play yourself.

Role-playing can be a powerful experience. Agree with your friend before you begin that you both have the right to stop the role-play at any point if you want to. At the end of the role-play, remind yourselves who you really are and spend some time talking about ordinary things.

Record below your feelings and thoughts about the conversation with your abuser. You may want to record details of the conversation as a reminder to yourself.

_____

_____

_____

_____

(continued)

_____

_____

_____

_____

_____

_____

Example of Graham's role-play confrontation

I felt sad and frightened at the same time. I began to feel my body pulsate and I was trembling. I knew my abuser was dead, but I began to tell her how she and the other bastards had screwed up my life. I knew I had the *power* to get rid of her and could shut her off at any time I wanted. I began to feel emotional and I could feel tears build up. I did not break down and cry and fight against it. I asked her if she thought I was so bad that she did the things she did and let others do it. She said she did nothing to me, and she said I was still the lying little bastard I had always been. I could feel the anger build up, and my head felt like it was going to explode, like a balloon.

The next time I did the exercise, I told her assertively that she was responsible along with the other bastards who repeatedly raped and abused me. I said, "I am sick of living my life believing it was my fault. Do you know I fucking hate you and I am glad you are dead. I never wanted to do those things that you made me do. I only did it willingly because I could not take the beatings if I didn't. All this is your fault, because you fucking started it. Go away and leave me and my family alone."

At first I was really scared, but then I asked myself, "Why?" I think I saw a person so pathetic that my feelings were slowly, gradually, getting better and stronger. For the first time in thirty-five years, I can see that although I was a child then, I am not a child anymore.

EXERCISE 8.6   WRITTEN CONFRONTATION

Purpose   To write a confrontation with your abuser as a way of feeling more empowered in relation to him or her and of challenging negative reactions aimed at you.

Use what you have written in Exercises 8.3 to 8.5 as the starting point to write a confrontation between you and your abuser. Write the confrontation in the form of a play or dialog. For example,

Me:	You raped me when I was eight.
Abuser:	I don't know what you are talking about.
Me:	Don't try to deny it. You raped me when I was a child, and you are responsible. What you did was very damaging to me, and illegal.

_____

_____

_____

_____

_____

_____

_____

_____

Survivors' comments

Today the world looks very different. I no longer immediately blame myself if things go wrong. I can step back and look at the situation from the perspective of "I'm OK" and assess my part in the problem. —*Rebecca*

With my brother as the abuser, I found it really hard to keep doing this exercise, because the fear I felt was too much. I was frightened of my brother, but I was also mad because he hurt me and he had no right to do that to me. Doing the confrontation exercise about my uncle was different. I felt more in control, which was nice. —*Lesley*

Standing Up to Others about the Abuse

Not only abusers react negatively when survivors speak out. You may have tried to talk about the abuse to family members, friends or people you thought might help you but had unhelpful reactions that left you feeling confused, guilty, upset or angry. Perhaps they didn't believe you or minimized what happened. Perhaps they blamed you for the abuse or tried to make you feel sorry for the abuser and guilty for speaking out. Learning to assert yourself about the abuse with other people can also be empowering and contribute to breaking the hold your abuser has over you. Use the confrontation exercises above to practice asserting yourself with others. Anthony used the written confrontation to assert himself (in his imagination) with his aunt about being abused by his uncle (her brother).

Example of Anthony's written confrontation with his aunt

Me: I don't like confronting you with this, but you already know that I went to the police and made a statement about your brother abusing me.

Aunt: Yes, I know you went to the police because your uncle told me they had him in for questioning. I have spoken to him about his abusing you, and he said he never abused you, and he thinks the world of you, and there is no way he could hurt you in that way.   **(Denial)**

Me: Well, he did, and he has caused me a lot of pain and suffering over the years, because I was only a child when it happened.

Aunt: So why did you wait this long if it happened when you were a child? Why didn't you tell anyone then?   **(Blaming)**

Me: Because I was scared that no one would believe me, and when it first started I was too young to know the what was happening.

Aunt: But when you did know what was happening, how come you let it go on? By then, you should have known he was doing something wrong, so you should have stopped it then.   **(Blaming)**

Me: I was ashamed of myself for letting it go on for so long, and I wondered what the consequences would be. Are you saying that I was as guilty as he was? Also, he still had power over me because when you are in your teens, you are still a boy. He was an adult, with adult authority over me, and you are told to trust adults. Do you understand that?

Aunt: Yes, I know that you are told to trust adults. But why go to the police now? Can't you drop it and forget about it? You know, if proceedings go ahead, he may end up in a psychiatric hospital again.   **(Guilt-tripping)**

Me: Don't forget, the police have picked him up before for abusing children, and he didn't end up in a psychiatric hospital then.

Aunt: Because they didn't press charges against him, because they had no proof that he had been abusing children.   **(Red herring)**

Me: Well, he abused me, I wouldn't lie about it, and I think he must have abused others. Put yourself in my shoes, knowing that he has abused and that he has caused a lot of pain and suffering and that he could still be abusing some child or teenager.

Challenge Your Own Negative Thoughts

Survivors who have had their abuse denied or minimized by their abuser or other people—or who have been blamed or threatened—often believe what they have been told.

What was said to them is what they learn to say to themselves. You may pretend that the abuse didn't happen **(denying)** or think it wasn't that bad **(minimizing).** You may be repeating to yourself what the abuser and others have said to you, but denying and minimizing can also be a way to cope with the painful reality of your experiences. You may **blame** yourself for the abuse—thinking you caused it or should have stopped it. You may also be excusing the abuser and be **guilt-tripping** yourself about the distress others might feel if you speak out about the abuse. Survivors who have been threatened by their abuser often believe the threat will be carried out if they talk about the abuse. They may internalize their abuser's threats and, in a way, may now be **threatening** *themselves* into remaining silent. For example, you may believe that if you speak out you will die, or that something terrible will happen to your family, or that the abuser will "know" and punish you for it. Sometimes survivors' fears that the threats will come true result in hallucinations about their abusers.

Try using the confrontation exercises to confront your own negative thoughts and respond assertively to them. Instead of confronting your abuser, use the exercises to confront the part of yourself that is denying, minimizing, blaming, excusing, guilt-tripping and threatening. Write down your own negative thoughts; for example, you might write, "I got into bed with him," on the left side of the page and then write an assertive response on the right. By learning to identify and challenge what you say to yourself, you can change your beliefs and start to break the internalized power of your abuser.

This chapter helps you focus on your feelings toward your abuser and to be clear about your abuser's responsibility for the abuse. The exercises build step by step to a confrontation exercise with your abuser in your imagination. Standing up to your abuser in your imagination is a way of feeling more empowered and breaking free from the hold he or she still has over you in your mind. The exercises in this chapter can also help you stand up to other people about the abuse, and to challenge your own negative thoughts. The next two chapters help you to continue to work on issues with others (chapter 9, "Mothers and Other Principal Caregivers") and yourself (chapter 10, "Childhood").

9

Mothers and
Other Principal Caregivers

Survivors of childhood sexual abuse frequently have strong negative or confusing feelings about people who were around them and didn't protect them from the abuse when it occurred. These feelings are often directed at their mothers, but may be directed at other people who did not sexually abuse them and who were supposed to take care of them, such as their stepmothers, adoptive or foster mothers, grandparents, fathers or aunts. In this chapter, the term "mother" is used to refer to the main caregiver who did not sexually abuse you.

Some children are sexually abused by their mothers. If this happened to you, work on your feelings toward your mother using the exercises in chapter 8, "Abusers," and use this chapter to work on your feelings about your other main caregiver, if you had one.

The purpose of this chapter is to help you understand the difficulties you may have in your relationship with your mother and to find ways of exploring and expressing the range of your feelings toward her. We also explore why some mothers don't protect their children from abuse and how this can make children feel they weren't worth protecting. You can do these exercises even if your mother or other main caregiver is dead or if you are no longer in contact with him or her.

Relationships with Mothers

Many people, whether or not they have been sexually abused, have problems in their relationships with their mothers. Childhood abuse can add specific difficulties to the child-mother relationship. The next two exercises are intended to help you focus on your current and childhood relationship with your mother and to help you think about how the sexual abuse may have caused difficulties in your relationship.

EXERCISE 9.1
RELATIONSHIP WITH MY MOTHER NOW

Purpose   To help you focus on the nature of your current relationship with your mother.

Read the following list and check all items that apply to you.

Applied to you?

My mother or main caregiver

Is dead   _____

Is alive but we are no longer in contact   _____

Still does not know about the abuse   _____

Now knows about the abuse and   _____

- supports me   _____

- rejects the abuser   _____

- still lives with the abuser   _____

- is still in contact with the abuser   _____

- does not acknowledge the abuse to me   _____

- blames me for it   _____

- does not believe me   _____

Toward me, my mother is

Abusive   _____

Angry   _____

Critical/judgmental   _____

Argumentative/quarrelsome   _____

Changeable   _____

Cold and distant   _____

Unsupportive   _____

Unassertive/passive   _____

Honest and assertive   _____

Understanding and sympathetic   _____

	Applied to you?
Supportive	_____
Warm and loving	_____

With my mother, I am

Abusive	_____
Angry	_____
Critical/judgmental	_____
Argumentative/quarrelsome	_____
Changeable	_____
Cold and distant	_____
Unsupportive	_____
Unassertive/passive	_____
Honest and assertive	_____
Understanding and sympathetic	_____
Supportive	_____
Warm and loving	_____

In your own words, describe below your current relationship with your mother.

_____

_____

_____

_____

_____

_____

_____

_____

_____

_____

_____

The Effects of Sexual Abuse on Your Relationship with Your Mother

Survivors may have problems in their relationships with their mothers for a number of reasons. The sexual abuse itself can create a barrier between mother and child because abused children often feel they cannot talk about the abuse and therefore need to remain at an emotional distance from their mothers. Abused children may also keep themselves at a distance from their mothers because they feel ashamed of what is happening to them and concerned about how their mothers might react if they found out. The relationship between a child and his or her mother may be particularly difficult if the abuser is the mother's partner. The abused child may feel he or she has betrayed the mother, or the mother might feel jealous of the child's "special" relationship with the abuser. Some mothers, although not sexually abusive, can be neglectful, uncaring or physically or emotionally abusive. This can increase the distress of children who are being sexually abused and make them feel more unloved, alone and unprotected.

EXERCISE 9.2   RELATIONSHIP WITH MY MOTHER WHEN I WAS A CHILD

Purpose   To describe how your mother behaved toward you when you were a child or young adult and to look at how the sexual abuse affected your relationship with her.

    The list below shows some of the ways mothers behave toward their children. The second list shows specific difficulties sexual abuse can add to the relationship. Read through the lists and check any items that applied to you. You may be able to add some others at the end.

Applies to you?

My mother was

Absent	_____
Cruel and mean	_____
Physically abusive	_____
Cold and distant	_____
Neglectful	_____
Showed no interest in me	_____
Affectionate	_____

	Applied to you?
Attentive/spent time with me	_____
Warm and loving	_____
Physically affectionate	_____

How the sexual abuse affected your relationship with your mother

As a child I thought my mother knew about the abuse	_____
I thought she was jealous of my relationship with the abuser	_____
I felt I was betraying my mother	_____
Keeping the abuse secret created a barrier between us	_____
I thought she should have protected me	_____
I was scared she would find out about the abuse	_____

My mother or main caregiver

Didn't notice signs of the abuse	_____
Ignored signs of the abuse	_____
Didn't listen or believe when I tried to tell	_____

Found out about the abuse when I was a child or a young person and

• didn't believe	_____
• supported the abuser	_____
• rejected me	_____
• blamed me	_____
• didn't stop it	_____

Write down any other difficulties relating to the sexual abuse that may have damaged your relationship with your mother.

_____

_____

_____

_____

_____

_____

_____

Having described your current relationship with your mother and identified the difficulties caused by the sexual abuse, read the next section to help you explore your feelings toward her.

Feelings toward Your Mother

Many people, whether they have been sexually abused or not, have a complex set of feelings toward their mother or mother figure. Survivors may feel love, hate, pity, guilt and resentment, or be overprotective, angry or jealous toward their mothers, or have any combination of feelings.

> Mom, I love you, I always will. But that doesn't mean I can't feel angry with you and let down by you.   —*Catherine*

Survivors may feel angry toward their mothers for not protecting them, or they may feel protective toward their mothers and be determined that they will never know about the abuse. Some of you may have spent your life trying to please your mother to win her approval. The complex and often conflicting feelings survivors have for their mothers can cause relationship difficulties.

EXERCISE 9.3
FEELINGS TOWARD YOUR MOTHER

Purpose   To help you explore and express your feelings toward your mother.

The exercises below suggest different ways of helping you become more aware of the whole range of your feelings toward your mother. You may wish to do all three of the following exercises, or one or two of them.

Letter to Your Mother

Write a letter to your mother expressing all the feelings you have toward her. *Do not send this letter.* The purpose of the letter is to help you become more aware of your feelings—it is *not* about actually communicating with her. This letter is *not* intended for your mother's eyes, so use the opportunity to write what you really feel. Express all your feelings, positive or negative, and try not to judge yourself for having "bad" or difficult feelings toward her. You may want to start by telling her why you are writing to her, how you felt about her at the time of the abuse and how you feel now.

Letter to my mother

Talking to a Chair

Some people find it easier to talk than write. Put two chairs next to each other and sit on one of them. Imagine your mother is sitting on the other. Position the chairs so you feel comfortable. Begin talking out loud to your mother. Some people find it easier to start by talking about everyday things, such as the kind of day they have had. When you feel ready, tell her how you feel about her, all your feelings—positive and negative. Remember, she cannot hear you, answer or be hurt by what you say, so feel free to say anything you want to. It may be difficult to start, so be patient and give yourself plenty of time.

Make notes in the speech bubble below about what you said.

Drawing Your Feelings

Some people prefer to express their feelings nonverbally; for example, by drawing or painting how they feel. Think about your mother and allow yourself to express your feelings with paint, pencils, crayons, salt-flour dough or clay, or any other art materials.

When you have done one or all of the three exercises above, try sitting quietly and becoming aware of how you are feeling *now*. Stay with your feelings for a short time, then find a way of expressing them. If you are sad or grieving, crying may help you release these feelings. You may feel like dancing, doing physical exercise, writing about how you feel, or contacting a friend or support person.

Lesley's example of writing to her mother

Lesley was sexually abused by her older brother and her uncle.

Dear Mom,

I am writing this letter to help me deal with my own feelings about you. For a long time, I hated you because I believe you knew I was being abused and you did nothing to help me. Now I feel sorry for you, knowing that you have to live with the guilt for the rest of your life. You're the one who has to look at my brother's face every day, not me.

You made me feel like I was not part of the family. I was the oddball. When I was younger, I hoped I was adopted because I could not believe I was hated so much. I wanted a family like my friends at school had. I would tell myself my real mother would come and get me.

When you made me have an abortion, I did not know what was happening. You sent me away with a person I did not like. After a month I was allowed to come home, but you never asked how I felt. It was brushed under the rug so none of the family would know anything about it. I was twelve years old, for God's sake. I was getting blamed for something I didn't know anything about. When I was about fourteen years old, I realized that what my brother and uncle were doing to me was not right. What could I have done, where could I have gone? You were never there as a mother for me. I just put up with it while you were in the next bedroom. Why didn't you ask me why I spent most of the night crying? You always said you were a light sleeper, so how come you never heard him walk past your bedroom to come into mine? Why did you let someone hurt me? You could have stopped all the pain I went through. My childhood was taken away from me, and you could have helped me.

Did you love me at all? I am glad you are out of my life, but I feel that somewhere deep down inside me there is still a little love.

I can't understand why you didn't believe me when I told you everything when I was twenty-five years old. You turned it around and said he was sleepwalking.

The only thing I still hate you for is not showing me how to love my kids. But I now know that I will try my hardest not to treat them in the way you treated me. It is very hard, but I am working on it. I am going to be a much better mother than you ever were. I am glad you are no longer part of my life.

Catherine's example of talking to a chair

Catherine was sexually abused by her father. She imagined her mother sitting on a chair and told her how she felt about her. Here are a few of the things she said.

> I love you, you'll always be my mom. You knew me better than anyone. So why didn't you ask me why I was so troubled? You must have noticed. There was such a change in me when my dad was in the house. You made a big mistake. I want you to know how angry I feel. I also want to thank you for the real love you gave me that made me feel special.

Survivor's comment

After writing the letter to my mother, I talked to a chair and I felt very angry with my mother because she wasn't there to listen to what I had to say. I got mad and kicked the chair and broke it. I got rid of a lot of anger. I suggest to other survivors who try this exercise that if you feel angry like I did, use something softer than a chair to take out your anger on!   —Lesley

Anger toward Mothers

Like Lesley, some of you may find that these exercises bring up strong feelings of anger toward your mother. Your mother may have abandoned, neglected, blamed or not believed you, or supported the abuser. She may not have noticed the abuse, or she may have known it was happening but did nothing to stop it. If your mother did not take care of you or protect you, you have the right to be upset and angry. Your feelings are important, and you may want to continue expressing your feelings outwardly by writing, talking to a chair again, or by doing something physical such as punching a pillow or getting some exercise.

You may not have felt nurtured and taken care of by your mother, so before you move on to the next exercise, spend some time being kind and gentle to yourself. Find a way of pampering yourself—perhaps by taking a bubble bath, eating a healthful meal or treating yourself.

Sometimes survivors blame (nonabusing) mothers for the sexual abuse. **The mother may be responsible for not protecting the child but the abuser is always responsible for the abuse.** The next section explores why some mothers don't protect their children.

Why Didn't My Mother Protect Me from the Abuse?

Mother, I feel mostly nothing toward you. In the past, I felt anger and pity. Maybe the pity was guilt. Guilt because I hated you. I remember when you were sick, I resented having to visit you. One day you couldn't get out of bed because of your bad back, and I stood there and ignored you. I couldn't make myself touch you. I felt so bad because I didn't help you. Maybe I resented helping you in your hour of need because you did nothing to help me.   —Sarah

Some mothers do not know that their children are being abused. Others do not protect their children, do not believe them when they try to tell about the abuse, or do not stop the abuse when they are aware it is happening. These behaviors can make survivors angry with their mothers for not protecting them—or confused, sad or perplexed about why their mothers didn't protect them.

Some survivors do not know how they feel about their mothers. Others cope with their feelings by being overprotective toward their mothers. If your mother knew about the abuse, or you thought she knew and she didn't protect you, then you might feel you deserved the abuse and were not worth protecting. Next we explore why mothers or other caregivers do not protect their children and emphasize that all children deserve to be protected.

Do any of the following statements apply to you?

1) My mother did not know about the abuse.
2) My mother didn't respond to signs that abuse was happening.

3) My mother knew about the abuse but did not stop it.
4) My mother didn't protect me when I told her about the abuse.

It may be hard to know if your mother knew about the abuse. You may feel sure she did know, when actually she was unaware of it. Or, you may be unconsciously protecting your mother by believing she didn't know about the abuse when actually she did know. You may never be sure if she knew or not, or why she didn't act to protect you, but the next exercises will help you explore these questions.

1. Mothers Who Don't Know

It may seem that mothers must know when their children are being abused, but some mothers have no idea. Abuse occurs in secret, and children are told to keep it secret. Abusers can be skillful at covering up signs of abuse and keeping children quiet. They are also good at manipulating people so they do not suspect anything; abusers can persuade a child's mother that they are caring people and the child is safe with them. Children often feel so ashamed of the abuse that they try to hide it from their mothers.

> I always felt so scared and frightened. I made it my life's work to be sure that nobody would ever find out what happened to me.   —Rebecca

You may have realized as a child that your mother did not know about the abuse, or it may come as a shock to realize now that your mother had no idea what was happening to you. As children, we expect our mothers to know how we are feeling and what is happening to us. It is hard to believe that the strong feelings you were experiencing did not show. Realizing that the abuse wasn't obvious to your mother or that the abuser may also have manipulated her may help you in your relationship with her.

However, you may still feel hurt or angry and think, "She *should* have known." You may feel guilty for feeling angry or resentful toward your mother because you believe you shouldn't have bad feelings about her. All children deserve to have a safe childhood in which they are protected from harm, and it is natural to feel angry with your mother if she did not protect you—even if she didn't know what was happening at the time and therefore could not have helped you.

Try to become aware of the whole range of your feelings toward your mother without judging yourself. You do not need to express these feelings to her, but it can help you to acknowledge them to yourself. It may also help you work through your feelings if you then express them outwardly, perhaps by doing Exercise 9.3 again.

2. Mothers Who Don't Respond to Signs of Abuse

Mom, You knew me better than anyone. You knew the real me. So why didn't you ask why I was so troubled? You must have noticed. There was such a change in me when my father was in the house. —*Catherine*

Children often show signs that they are being abused (we will look at these "silent ways of telling" in the next chapter): A mother may see the abuser and child in suspicious circumstances or a child may have given hints about the abuse. Why don't some mothers realize or acknowledge that the abuse is happening?

EXERCISE 9.4 WHY SOME MOTHERS DON'T RESPOND TO SIGNS OF ABUSE

Purpose   To help you explore the reasons your mother didn't notice or act on signs of the abuse.

The list below gives some of the reasons mothers may not recognize signs of ongoing abuse. You may not know if these reasons applied to your mother or not. Read the list and check items that might have applied to your situation. You may be able to add new ones at the end of the list.

Why some mothers don't respond to signs of abuse	Applied to you?
The abuse always happened when my mother wasn't there.	_____
She was wrapped up in her own problems at the time and didn't notice me.	_____
She was always out of the house.	_____
She was sick a lot and wasn't around to see it happening.	_____
She was always drunk and didn't notice anything.	_____
The abuser was expert at covering it up.	_____
She was not aware of sexual abuse or its signs.	_____
The abuser told her I was just behaving badly.	_____

(continued)

Why some mothers don't respond to signs of abuse	Applied to you?
She thought something else was causing the changes in my behavior.	_____
The abuser told her we were just playing.	_____
She just thought I was being moody.	_____
She couldn't believe her own child was being abused—"It only happens in other families."	_____
She loved the abuser and couldn't imagine he or she could do it.	_____

Pauline's example

> Some of the abuse happened in other people's houses, or "trusted" people used to take me and my brothers out to places where they abused me. At home, my mother was the victim of all kinds of abuse from my father and probably didn't even know what planet she was on. I know she was powerless where my father was concerned—like a lot of other people. My mother couldn't protect me because of her own circumstances with my father, and she was trying to protect all her children from his violence and emotional abuse. I don't think the thought of sexual abuse even entered her mind. She had much bigger worries at the time—fearing for her own and her children's welfare and maybe even their lives. After doing this exercise, I now believe my mother could not have known about the sexual abuse. I don't blame anybody now except the abusers themselves.

Survivors' comments

It showed me that any feelings are OK. I was hurt that my mother didn't protect me at the time, but I also felt so sorry for her because she tried to be a perfect mother, and she stood by me when she could. She didn't know about the sexual abuse then and I know she has gone through hell since she found out and has felt so guilty that she didn't protect me. She has talked to me about it and apologized and has shown me how much she regrets being unaware of the abuse at the time. I forgive her with all my heart.   —Pauline

It helped to see my mom's side of things, and that reduced the anger I feel toward her. I feel the need to let her know I'm not angry with her anymore.   —Catherine

When children do show signs of abuse, the signs may be almost undetectable changes in their behavior or very noticeable changes. The reasons mothers do not act when their children show signs of abuse include

- They do not notice the signs.
- They see changes in their children but misinterpret them.
- They see the signs but deny to themselves that abuse is happening.

These reasons are discussed below.

Mothers Who Don't Notice the Signs

Some mothers do not notice signs that their children are in distress. They may not have seen the signs because they were sick or not around when the abuse was happening. Other mothers were involved in abusive relationships themselves, had drug or alcohol problems, or were so wrapped up in their own problems or their own lives that they failed to notice signs of abuse in their children.

Mothers Who Misinterpret Signs of Abuse

Catherine's behavior changed when her father began sexually abusing her. Catherine's mother did notice changes in her when her father was in the house but thought Catherine was scared of him because he was an intimidating man. It never occurred to Catherine's mother that Catherine was distressed because her father was sexually abusing her.

Survivors' mothers may notice changes in their children's behavior but interpret them in different ways, without considering sexual abuse as a possible cause. They might believe a child was bedwetting or having nightmares because of problems at school. As children, both Pauline and Catherine thought their mothers must have noticed signs of the abuse and consequently felt angry toward them. Both mothers noticed their daughters were upset and disturbed, but attributed this to other circumstances in their lives. Pauline and Catherine now believe their mothers did not know about the sexual abuse when they were children. This has helped them in their current relationships with their mothers.

Public awareness of child sexual abuse is very recent, and your mother may have had little knowledge or awareness about sexual abuse. She may have noticed the changes in your behavior or mood but not recognized them as signs of abuse and was therefore not in a position to protect you.

Mothers Who Deny Signs of Abuse

People often cope with an event that feels unbearable by telling themselves it is not really happening. Most mothers would find it easier to believe "abuse only happens in other families" than believe it could be happening in their own. Some mothers may notice signs of sexual abuse but are unable to bear the thought that their children are being abused. Mothers who deny abuse in this way do not act to protect their children because they are not consciously aware that abuse is happening.

Some mothers were sexually abused themselves as children but never told anyone or received help. They may have pushed the abuse out of their minds or persuaded themselves it didn't happen. A mother who denies her own abuse may find it difficult to see that her children are being abused. If she recognizes her children's abuse, she must accept that she was abused also. Such a realization may be terrifying. Mothers who are in this situation may deny to themselves that their children are suffering abuse, rather than deliberately ignore it.

If your mother did not respond to the signs of abuse, for whatever reason, you may have felt you were not worth caring for. Remember, all children have a right to a safe childhood, and you also deserved to be protected as a child.

3. Mothers Who Know and Don't Stop the Abuse

It may be difficult to know if your mother didn't notice the abuse or if she did know about it and did not act. However, sometimes it is clear that mothers know about the abuse. They may actually see the abuse happening or have been told about it. If your mother knew about the abuse, you have probably struggled to understand why she didn't stop it. The next exercise helps you think about why your mother failed to protect you.

EXERCISE 9.5
WHY SOME MOTHERS DON'T STOP THE ABUSE

Purpose   To explore the reasons mothers do not stop abuse and to emphasize that you did deserve to be protected.

Read the list below, which suggests reasons why some mothers don't stop abuse. See if you can add others, and check any that applied to you.

Why some mothers don't stop the abuse	Applied to you?
She was too concerned about herself to care about anyone else	_____
She had been abused herself and didn't realize abuse could be stopped or she thought abuse was "normal"	_____

Why some mothers don't stop the abuse　　　　　　**Applied to you?**

She was afraid of the abuser　　　　　　　_____

She felt powerless to stop the abuse　　　　　　_____

She didn't trust the authorities and wouldn't tell them　　_____

She didn't want the abuser to get into trouble　　　_____

She was financially dependent on the abuser　　　_____

She was emotionally dependent on the abuser　　　_____

She was scared of breaking up the family　　　　_____

She couldn't cope with the scandal if it
　came out in the open　　　　　　　　　_____

She didn't want to rock the boat　　　　　　_____

The abuser didn't have sex with her when
　I was being abused　　　　　　　　　_____

The abuser was kinder to her when I was being abused　_____

She was obsessed with the abuser and would
　let him do anything　　　　　　　　　_____

She blamed me for the abuse and thought
　I should stop it　　　　　　　　　　_____

She blamed me for the abuse and thought I deserved it　_____

_____　　_____

_____　　_____

_____　　_____

_____　　_____

_____　　_____

_____　　_____

_____　　_____

Example

I don't think my mother knew that my uncle was abusing me because
it happened at his house, but I believe my mother knew I was being
abused by my brother. The reasons she didn't stop it may have been

- She couldn't believe her son would do something like that.
- She did not want her son to get in trouble.
- She was probably abused herself and couldn't handle it.
- She thought I'd led him on, so I deserved what I got. —Lesley

She couldn't see that what my stepfather was doing to me was wrong.
—*Danny*

Some mothers do not stop the abuse when they know about it. There are different reasons for this. Their attention and concern may have been focused on themselves instead of on their children's needs. Some mothers do not feel powerful enough to stop the abuse themselves and may believe that other people also are unable to stop it. Some may turn a blind eye to the abuse because they are afraid of the consequences of trying to stop it, while others may be protecting the abuser or their relationship with the abuser. Whatever the reason, it was your mother's responsibility to try to protect you.

4. Mothers Who Don't Protect when Told about the Abuse

Most survivors would not have been able to tell their mothers about the abuse. Some children and adults do tell their mothers and receive supportive and protective responses, while others receive negative reactions. It is damaging to children and adults to tell, receive a negative response and remain unprotected.

EXERCISE 9.6 NEGATIVE RESPONSES FROM MOTHER AT DISCLOSURE

Purpose To look at the negative responses survivors sometimes receive from their mothers at disclosure.

Here is a list of some of the negative responses that survivors have received on disclosure. Read the list and check any responses you had.

Your mother	Happened to you?
Ignored what you said	
Minimized the abuse, and	
• said the abuser was only playing	_____
• said the abuser was tickling you	_____
• said the abuser was only being affectionate	_____
Blamed you, and	
• slapped you	_____

Happened to you?

- called you a slut/bad   _____
- said you tried to steal her partner   _____
- had you taken from home so she could stay
  with the abuser (for example, into foster care,
  to a hospital, to relatives)   _____
- told you to leave home   _____

Did not believe you, and

- called you a liar   _____
- said you were crazy/mentally ill   _____
- said the abuser would not do anything like that   _____

Write down the response you received.

_____

_____

_____

_____

_____

_____

_____

How did this response make you feel?

_____

_____

_____

_____

_____

_____

_____

Some adult survivors believe they told their mothers about the abuse when they were children, but when they looked back at what they said, they realized they had only hinted at the abuse. For example, if a child says, "I don't like the way my stepdad plays with me," the mother may have believed the stepfather was only playing roughly with the child.

However, the child is left feeling upset that the mother did not react by protecting him or her. If you did tell, it may help you to think back to what you actually said. Pauline thought she had told her mother about the abuse by her grandfather, but thinking back, she realized she had not been clear:

> I didn't tell my mom clearly what grandad did to me. I was scared she might think I'd led him on. She couldn't act on what had happened because I know I wasn't direct and I didn't tell her the whole truth.

Pauline also realized that even if she had been explicit, her mother may still have been unable to protect her:

> If I had told her the whole truth, she may or may not have acted on it.

Survivors often blame themselves for the abuse because they did not tell, but some children are left unprotected even when they do tell someone they trust.

You may have been explicit and clear and still your mother did not listen to, protect or believe you. She may have believed the abuser if that person denied abusing. Some mothers do not respond appropriately to disclosures of abuse for reasons that are similar to those given in the lists in Exercises 9.4 and 9.5. Look through those lists again and see if they help you understand why your mother didn't protect you when you tried to tell.

Summary: Why Some Mothers Do Not Protect Their Children

Sometimes there are no signs that children are being abused, so their mothers don't know that abuse is happening. Where children show signs of being upset or disturbed, their mothers may genuinely believe the upset is caused by something else, or they don't know why the child is disturbed.

If your mother did not realize you were being abused, then she could not protect you. However, as a child you may have felt unprotected by your mother, or you may feel angry with her now. It may help you in your current relationship with your mother if you accept and work through these feelings.

Sometimes mothers take no notice of the signs, deny the abuse is happening or know about the abuse and do not stop it. Mothers who behave in these ways are responsible for not protecting their children.

If you were unprotected, you may believe you were not lovable or you were not worth protecting. Our exercise asked you to explore why your mother didn't stop the abuse. The purpose was to help you understand that your mother didn't help you because of *her own* self-interest or situation. It was *not* because you did or did not do something or because you were not worth taking care of. You *did* deserve to be protected.

Whether or not your mother knew about the abuse, you may still feel sad, angry or confused about why you were not protected. If your mother knew about the abuse or ignored the signs, you may still wonder why she did not stop it. The next exercise helps you continue to explore your questions about why she didn't protect you. It also helps you look for some answers.

EXERCISE 9.7
LETTERS TO AND FROM YOUR MOTHER

Purpose   To help you understand more about why your mother did not protect you and to help you see that her nonresponse had to do with her, not you. You were worth protecting.

Letter to your mother

Write a letter to your mother (do not send the letter) asking her why she did not protect you from the abuse. You may want to ask your mother why she didn't notice or react to signs that the abuse was happening (for example, changes in your mood or behavior, suspicious circumstances, hints you might have made), or why she didn't listen to or believe you if you did tell.

Your Mother's Situation at the Time of the Abuse

You may understand more about why your mother did not protect you from the abuse if you think about her situation at the time of your abuse.

Think about the following:

- How old was she then?
- How many children did she have?
- What other responsibilities did she have?
- Did she have a job?
- What kind of relationship did she have with her partner (if she had one)?
- What kind of relationship did she have with your abuser? (*Note:* Her partner and your abuser may be the same person.)
- What else was happening in her life at the time?

Letter from Your Mother

You may now understand more about your mother's situation at the time of your abuse. Write a reply to the letter you wrote above *as if you were your mother* and write about the reasons your mother did not notice the abuse or did not stop it. (The examples that follow this exercise may help.)

Examples

Sarah's letters

Dear Mother,

I can come up with all kinds of reasons why you didn't protect me but deep down, I know why. You just didn't care. I was a handful and you were too busy surviving your own shitty life. But I still wonder what your reasons were. Why didn't you protect me? Why didn't you love me? I have asked you this before and your answer was, "No one could love you, they couldn't get near you, you were a wild animal." When you told me this, didn't you ever wonder why? Didn't you feel guilty?
—Sarah

Dear Sarah,

I was unable to stop your abuse because I wasn't aware of it most of the time. I suppose I was too selfish and too busy trying to survive myself. To acknowledge it would have caused me too much distress. I felt helpless. I know our family life was a joke, but it was the only normality I knew. I didn't want to rock the boat because I learned a long time ago that keeping silent was the only way of keeping the family together. I pretended it was your fault, and it didn't matter because you were so disturbed and damaged anyway. I am guilty of putting my need for a family before your need to be protected. I can't acknowledge the guilt or shame because I know it will consume me and destroy my world. I would have to acknowledge that I am a failure as a mother and a human being.

Your world is so far apart from mine. What you have is what I always wanted. I want to say that I do love you and am proud to call you my daughter. I know I don't show it, because I know you will reject me the way I rejected you. I am sorry I did not protect you. I suffer now, knowing that you do not care for me like a daughter should. You could say what goes around comes around. I got what I deserved.
—Mother

Sarah's comments

This exercise moved me. I felt a warmth toward my mother I haven't felt before. I also felt sad writing this. I may be getting her to say what I want her to say. Maybe I'm denying or justifying my mother's actions, but I now understand how helpless she was. I realize that the only people to blame are the abusers.

Maya's letters

Maya was abused by her mother and felt unprotected by her stepfather. She wrote this letter to him.

> To my stepfather: I know what my mother was doing to me when I was a child and so do you—no matter how much you deny it. Why didn't you help me? You turned a blind eye to my abuse because you were afraid of my mother's violence and because she told you to stay out of it because I wasn't your child. How could you have colluded with her and made me feel I was bad and worthless when I loved you so much? How could you?

> Dear Maya,

> I know you hold me responsible for not stopping the abuse by your mother and I don't blame you. Please forgive me—none of it was your fault.
> I was afraid of your mom's rages and violent outbursts. I just didn't know what to do. I thought if I stayed quiet and calm it would pacify her and sometimes it did. Your mom would cry bitterly afterward and vow she would never hurt you again. She was very damaged by her own childhood and took it out on you.
> I have many regrets about it now and wish I had done more to help you. I am truly sorry.

> Love,
> Dad xxxxxxx

After doing these exercises, some of you, like Sarah, may have a better understanding of why your mothers did not notice or stop the abuse. Others may find it difficult to put themselves in their mothers' position or, like Lesley, may not be able to think of any answers:

> I have written to my mother but I can't write back to myself from her. I feel unable to answer my questions about why she didn't protect me. I don't know the answers. No matter how hard I try, I can't answer them.

Lesley's mother arranged for her to have an abortion when she was only twelve years old. Lesley knew her mother must have known she was being raped and finds it very difficult to understand how her mother could have left her so unprotected. Some of you may never know why your mother did not stop the abuse.

It is sad that many children are abused by a trusted adult and are not protected by their mother or main caregiver. If this has happened to you, you feel sad, betrayed, confused, angry or have other strong feelings, and it may help you to find your own way of expressing these feelings. **It is important to understand that you were very unfortunate to be in that situation, but it was not your fault. You deserved to be protected. If your mother knew about the abuse and failed to protect you, for whatever reason, she is responsible for her neglect. Every child has a right to be protected from abuse.**

Changing Your Relationship with Your Mother

In this chapter, we have focused on exploring your feelings toward your mother. You may want to make changes in your relationship with her now. You may understand more about her circumstances at the time of the abuse and be able to let go of resentment or negative feelings. You may be able to allow yourself to have a closer or easier relationship.

You may decide you want to talk to your mother about the abuse or about how you feel. This could be helpful, but it could also be difficult, because your mother may not believe you or respond as you expect or want her to. If you want to talk to your mother about the abuse, be sure to prepare yourself for all possible outcomes by talking it through with someone first or role-playing what might happen. This kind of preparation is important.

Some mothers persist in blaming or disbelieving their children or in treating them badly. Your mother may have treated you badly over the years, and over time you may have learned to put up with it. No one deserves to be treated badly, and you do not have to accept being used or abused. Everyone has the right to decide how much contact they want with another person, including their mothers, and to choose to break off contact with someone who is abusing or upsetting them. Reducing or breaking off contact with your mother can be a painful choice and needs to be thought about carefully. However, this is a positive choice for some adult survivors of childhood sexual abuse.

> After writing to my mother and talking to the chair, I cried and felt relieved. I also felt helpless, knowing she could never accept what I say. I have started to come to terms with this and have realized a happy ending isn't possible. I still have occasional contact with them, but I now have a separate life from my family and my mother. —*Sarah*

It can be difficult to make changes in the important and longstanding relationship between you and your mother. Reading the chapter on mothers in our book *Surviving Childhood Sexual Abuse* may help you think about what you want to change in your relationship with your mother and how to approach making the changes. Counseling can also help you resolve your feelings toward your mother and work on your relationship with her.

In this chapter, you have explored your relationship with your mother or main caregiver and perhaps become aware of how vulnerable and unprotected you were as a child. The next chapter helps you think again about your situation as a child and encourages you to look back with sympathy on the child you were.

10

Childhood

> When I was a child, I used to take drugs, drink alcohol, cut myself and run away from home. The adults around me thought I was a bad girl and I was behaving badly to get attention. Yes I was, but no one asked me if I had a problem, so I'd just do it even more to get more attention. Why didn't they just ask? I needed support, care and comfort and I didn't receive any, so I took drugs instead. What I wanted was love.
> —Lesley

Children who are being abused need to find ways of dealing with their feelings and coping with what is happening to them. They often express their distress through changes in mood or behavior. Unfortunately, adults may only see these children as behaving badly or being disruptive and may punish or blame them. The children in turn may come to believe that they are bad or that something is wrong with them. Survivors can grow up thinking they were bad children as well as blaming themselves for the abuse and feeling ashamed of the sexual experiences their abusers subjected them to. As adults they often have negative feelings toward themselves as children, and have the same feelings toward themselves as adults.

In chapter 2 you saw how your problems as an adult were related to your past experiences. This chapter is intended to help you look back at your childhood and understand that many of your feelings and behaviors as a child were a response to the abuse. The exercises here are also designed to enable you to begin to communicate with and take care of the child you were.

Many survivors find it difficult and painful to look back on childhood. They are afraid of being overwhelmed by feelings of despair, loneliness, anger and shame, among others. The exercises in this chapter help you think about yourself as a child with your current adult knowledge and understanding. It is important that you follow the suggestions in chapter 1 and keep yourself at a safe emotional distance from your childhood experiences as you work through these exercises.

Silent Ways of Telling

As we discussed in chapter 5, most children do not tell anyone when they are being abused because they are manipulated by the abuser and feel other pressures to keep quiet. Although they usually do not *say* anything, the behavior of abused children often changes in some way. Children, like adults, have to find ways of coping with bad experiences, and they may express their pain or confusion by wetting the bed, having nightmares, becoming moody, being disruptive at school or by eating a lot, for example.

> As a child, I was naughty and anxious and exhibited strange behavior, hoping that people would figure out I was being abused—just so I wouldn't have to tell them and be punished for telling. —*Eileen*

Such mood and behavior changes are the child's silent cries for help, and in *Surviving Childhood Sexual Abuse* we refer to them as "silent ways of telling." Children usually find some way of expressing their distress or crying out for help when they cannot ask for help directly. The following exercises are designed to help you become aware of the kinds of problems you had as a child and to see that you shared these problems with other children who were sexually abused.

EXERCISE 10.1 SILENT WAYS OF TELLING

Purpose To look at the ways children show they are upset or disturbed and help you see that your moods and behaviors were ways of expressing your distress.

The list below identifies mood and behavior changes that abused children commonly display. Showing any of these problems does not mean a child has been sexually abused. The behaviors indicate that a child might be upset or disturbed by *something*—it may be sexual abuse or it may be any other childhood experience.

- Read the list and see if you can add any other ways that children might express their distress or cope with abuse.
- Look back at yourself as a child. Check any of the behaviors listed that applied to you. Add any of your own behaviors and feelings that are not given.

Childhood Signs of Distress

The following signs suggest a child is being sexually abused:

Applied to you?	Yes	A little	No
Displaying too much sexual knowledge for their age	_____	_____	_____
Inappropriate sexual behavior; e.g., tongue kissing	_____	_____	_____
Writing stories about sex or abuse	_____	_____	_____
Drawing pictures about sex or abuse	_____	_____	_____
Sexually transmitted diseases	_____	_____	_____

The following signs do not necessarily mean a child is being sexually abused. They do indicate that something may be upsetting or disturbing the child:

Applied to you?	Yes	A little	No
Eating problems			
Refusing to eat	_____	_____	_____
Overeating	_____	_____	_____
Compulsive eating	_____	_____	_____
Binge-eating	_____	_____	_____
Bingeing and vomiting (bulimia nervosa)	_____	_____	_____
Abusing laxatives	_____	_____	_____
Anorexia nervosa	_____	_____	_____
Excreting problems			
Wetting	_____	_____	_____
Bed-wetting	_____	_____	_____
Retaining urine	_____	_____	_____
Soiling	_____	_____	_____
Constipation	_____	_____	_____
Diarrhea	_____	_____	_____
Retaining feces	_____	_____	_____
Smearing feces	_____	_____	_____
Changes in behavior or mood			
Withdrawing from people	_____	_____	_____
Not communicating	_____	_____	_____
Fearful of being alone with particular people	_____	_____	_____
Not making close friends	_____	_____	_____
Trying to be perfect	_____	_____	_____
Depression	_____	_____	_____

(continued)

Applied to you?	*Yes*	*A little*	*No*
Anxiety	‾‾‾	‾‾‾	‾‾‾
Phobias	‾‾‾	‾‾‾	‾‾‾
Nightmares	‾‾‾	‾‾‾	‾‾‾
Difficulty sleeping	‾‾‾	‾‾‾	‾‾‾
Constantly tired	‾‾‾	‾‾‾	‾‾‾
Suicide attempts	‾‾‾	‾‾‾	‾‾‾
Obsessional behavior or thoughts	‾‾‾	‾‾‾	‾‾‾
Tantrums	‾‾‾	‾‾‾	‾‾‾
Clinging to adults	‾‾‾	‾‾‾	‾‾‾
Acting younger than your age	‾‾‾	‾‾‾	‾‾‾
Running away	‾‾‾	‾‾‾	‾‾‾
Disruptive behavior at home	‾‾‾	‾‾‾	‾‾‾
Disruptive behavior at school	‾‾‾	‾‾‾	‾‾‾
Truancy	‾‾‾	‾‾‾	‾‾‾
Underachievement at school	‾‾‾	‾‾‾	‾‾‾
Overachievement at school	‾‾‾	‾‾‾	‾‾‾
Bullying	‾‾‾	‾‾‾	‾‾‾
Fighting	‾‾‾	‾‾‾	‾‾‾
Aggressive or violent behavior	‾‾‾	‾‾‾	‾‾‾
Stealing	‾‾‾	‾‾‾	‾‾‾
Frequent illnesses; for example, stomachache, rashes, sore genitals	‾‾‾	‾‾‾	‾‾‾
Frequent "accidents"	‾‾‾	‾‾‾	‾‾‾
Self-mutilation or self-abuse; for example, slashing, scratching	‾‾‾	‾‾‾	‾‾‾
Alcohol, drug abuse	‾‾‾	‾‾‾	‾‾‾
_____	‾‾‾	‾‾‾	‾‾‾
_____	‾‾‾	‾‾‾	‾‾‾
_____	‾‾‾	‾‾‾	‾‾‾
_____	‾‾‾	‾‾‾	‾‾‾
_____	‾‾‾	‾‾‾	‾‾‾
_____	‾‾‾	‾‾‾	‾‾‾
_____	‾‾‾	‾‾‾	‾‾‾

Examples

Annabelle

Wanting to be thin.
Having sore throats and chest pains.

Disliking surprises.
Feeling protective of my mother.
Talking about my abuse in story form.
Avoiding sex education classes.
Being solemn.
Scared of the "bye-bye man" who came at night.
Always being alert/on guard.

Graham

Always apologizing.
Banging my head.
Crying and depressed.
Slashing my wrists and overdosing.
Hiding from people.
Withdrawing from life.
No appetite.

Karen

I really wanted to be liked, so I tried to be perfect. I wanted to please everyone. When I was seven, I did all the housework and all the shopping. I tried to stay away from home and camped out at my friends' houses.

Lesley

I felt alone. It was a way of life to let people touch you whenever they wanted to. I let boys and men have sex with me even when I didn't want to.

Danny

I used to wet my bed and I began making my bed to hide the fact because I'd be yelled at. My mother accused me of doing it deliberately. She said I was too lazy to get up at night to go to the bathroom. As though I'd lie there wetting myself and lying in a pool of urine all night on purpose!

In junior high, I would defecate in the washbasins, on toilet seats and on the floor of the toilets.

I stole things in and out of the home.

Extreme cases of vandalism in and out of our house.

General bad behavior, such as making false 9-1-1 calls.

Suffering intense headaches/migraines twice a week.

Survivors' comments

Seeing the list of "silent ways of telling" made my problems more acceptable to me, because other children acted in similar ways. —*Karen*

I was reluctant to start writing. I was feeling tense and panicky at the thought of remembering what I was like as a child. I had to make myself feel safe first by waiting until I was alone in the house and climbing into my sleeping bag with my favorite pillow. I became aware of the long list of problems I had as a child and how I was crying out for help but no one heard me. I let myself feel upset and angry and managed not to space out (my usual way of coping). It helped me understand that my behavior as a child was an indication of distress and was not because I was bad. I feel sad that there wasn't anyone there to help me at the time. —*Maya*

I hadn't realized the extent of the problem. Doing this exercise linked what I had considered separate things, and a pattern formed that shows I was screaming for help. I thought I was just a bad boy with all this delinquent behavior. It gave me some understanding and sympathy for my actions, for which I had been labeled bad and naughty. I felt angry at adults, even the ones I'd previously thought were all right. Adults are crap, they have no idea of a child's psychology. They all punish kids without finding out what is behind the behavior. No one listens to children. They're treated like second-class citizens. For teenagers, it's even worse. Adults suck! —*Danny*

I realized how many ways I'd tried to tell but wasn't noticed. I felt upset and cried. —*Pauline*

Why Do Children Behave in These Ways?

Unfortunately, when children behave in the ways listed above, adults around them often perceive them as naughty, bad, stubborn or ungrateful. They may even be seen as "mentally ill." Survivors have said that as children they were told they were crazy, bad, silly, stupid, weird, unreasonable, a spoiled little brat, evil, possessed by the devil, disruptive. Children who grow up being told these things soon begin to believe it and think that their "silent ways of telling" prove how bad they really are. They may even believe they were abused because they were bad. In fact, their behaviors were ways of expressing how bad they were feeling or were ways of coping with what was happening in their lives.

EXERCISE 10.2 HOW I BEHAVED AS A CHILD

Purpose   To increase your awareness of why you felt and behaved the way you did as a child.

- Look back on your childhood and try to see that you were not bad but a child in distress, a child trying to survive abuse who was crying for help.
- Look back on your childhood and choose a time that was difficult for you. What did you think about yourself? How did you feel? How was your behavior affected by the abuse? Think about why you acted in these ways and fill in the bubbles below. The examples that follow may help you. If you prefer, write an account of how you were affected and why.

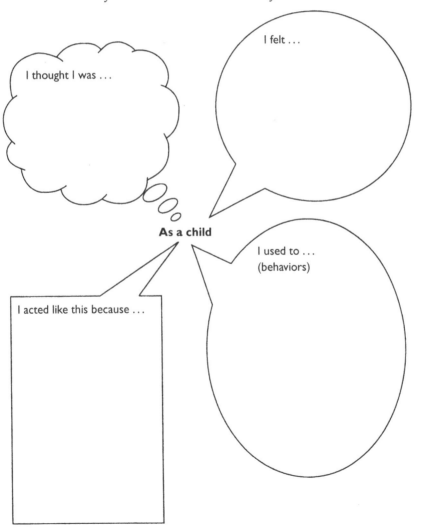

I thought I was . . .

I felt . . .

As a child

I used to . . .
(behaviors)

I acted like this because . . .

Examples

Danny

Danny was physically and emotionally abused as a child. He went into foster care because of behavior problems when he was thirteen years old.

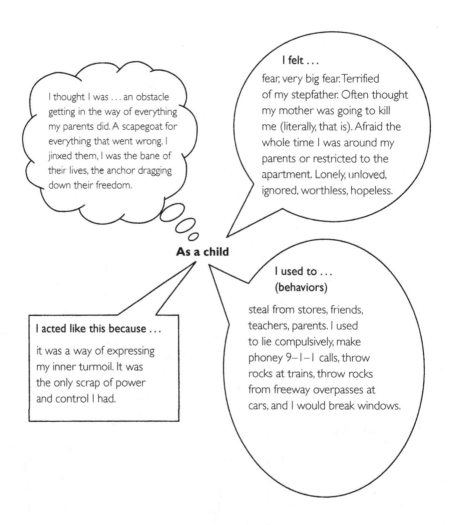

I thought I was ... an obstacle getting in the way of everything my parents did. A scapegoat for everything that went wrong. I jinxed them, I was the bane of their lives, the anchor dragging down their freedom.

I felt ...

fear, very big fear. Terrified of my stepfather. Often thought my mother was going to kill me (literally, that is). Afraid the whole time I was around my parents or restricted to the apartment. Lonely, unloved, ignored, worthless, hopeless.

As a child

I acted like this because ...

it was a way of expressing my inner turmoil. It was the only scrap of power and control I had.

I used to ... (behaviors)

steal from stores, friends, teachers, parents. I used to lie compulsively, make phoney 9–1–1 calls, throw rocks at trains, throw rocks from freeway overpasses at cars, and I would break windows.

Maya

Maya was sexually, physically and emotionally abused by her mother. Her stepfather and the other adults around her ignored what was happening.

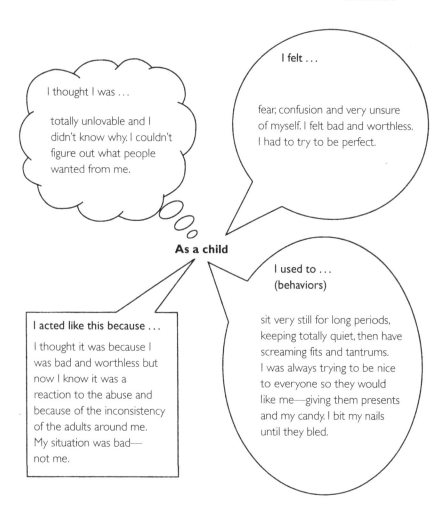

I thought I was . . .

totally unlovable and I didn't know why. I couldn't figure out what people wanted from me.

I felt . . .

fear, confusion and very unsure of myself. I felt bad and worthless. I had to try to be perfect.

As a child

I acted like this because . . .

I thought it was because I was bad and worthless but now I know it was a reaction to the abuse and because of the inconsistency of the adults around me. My situation was bad— not me.

I used to . . . (behaviors)

sit very still for long periods, keeping totally quiet, then have screaming fits and tantrums. I was always trying to be nice to everyone so they would like me—giving them presents and my candy. I bit my nails until they bled.

Survivors' comments

It helped me highlight the links between different aspects of my life. I hadn't realized how I had felt as a child or how it had had such an effect on me as an adult. —*Danny*

Focusing on how I felt was helpful. I don't think I have ever been asked how I felt as a child before. —*Rebecca*

I was only three years old when I was sexually abused, so it was difficult for me to do this exercise. I had only feelings, and no vocabulary to go with them. It made me realize I wasn't a moody child—I had behavioral problems because of my traumatic situation. I felt sympathy for the little girl, like she was a relative I loved very much, but she wasn't actually me. —*Catherine*

Communicating with Yourself as a Child

During your childhood you may have felt alone and misunderstood. You may have tried to tell but no one listened, believed or supported you. You may have expressed your distress in the ways you behaved, but unfortunately no one understood. The next exercise helps you communicate with and support the child you were. It is an opportunity for the child you were to talk about his or her feelings, and for you as an adult to listen, understand and be ready to help and care for the child. The child you were is sometimes referred to as your "inner child" or the "child within."

If you were a lonely, isolated or angry child, it may be difficult for you to make contact with the child at first. Think about how you would have liked a caring adult to approach you when you were a child. What would you have liked that person to say to you?

This is a powerful exercise. You may feel like a child again when you do this exercise. Your handwriting might even revert to a child's handwriting. If you feel overwhelmed by your feelings, take a break and take care of yourself, get some support or return to chapter 1.

EXERCISE 10.3
LETTERS TO YOUR INNER CHILD

Purpose   To communicate with the child you were and to support and comfort him or her.

1) Think of an incident or a time as a child when you were unhappy. This does not have to be during the time you were being abused.

Write a letter to yourself as the child you were, from the adult you are now. Try to make contact with him or her. Tell the child you are an adult who will listen and believe and will try to understand what is happening. Write your letter in simple language, the language a child could understand. If you had a nickname as a child, you may want to use it in your letter.

Dear _____,

2) Write a reply to yourself as you are now from this child. Try to remember how you felt as a child and what you would have liked from an adult. You may want to write about how you were feeling, what was happening to you, the things you didn't understand.

Dear _____,

3) Continue writing letters to and from yourself as a child so the adult part of yourself is able to support and accept the child you were and the child feels comforted.

As an adult, you might try to explain to the child how he or she was not to blame for the abuse and did not deserve to be abused. The adult may be able to help the child understand his or her moods, feelings and behaviors. As you continue writing letters, you may be able to get closer to the child who felt unloved and alone and offer the child love and support. You can help the child realize he or she is no longer alone. Comforting the child could take some time, so keep returning to this letter-writing exercise over the following months.

Examples

Maya's letters

Dear Little Maya,

I am so sorry for all the bad things that happened. None of them were your fault, and you didn't deserve to be treated like that. I am sorry I didn't like you before and thought you were a nuisance. I was wrong and I will try to make up for it now. When I look at your photograph, I see a beautiful, tiny child with pretty brown eyes and dimpled cheeks. I just want to pick you up and hold you, take care of you, have fun with you. We will do all of these things together. We will walk hand in hand and I will show you how lovable you are and always were.

You are not alone now.

I love you,

Big Maya

Dear Big Maya,

Thank you very much for your letter. It means everything to me to know you care about me. I felt ugly and unwanted before. It is so good to be told I am beautiful and that you want to be with me. I can't believe it yet, though, so you will have to go slowly because I am not used to trusting people.

Little Maya

Sarah's letters

Sarah's parents neglected her, and her brother sexually abused her, as did other people outside the family. As a child, she was isolated and moody. Sarah had to write several letters to her child self before the child was able to respond. These are extracts from some of the later letters.

> Dear child,
>
> You may find this hard to believe, but I love you and care about you. It isn't because you are no good that the people around you aren't interested in you. You deserve better—they should show you kindness, understanding and warmth. To help you feel better, I would like you to tell me some of the things that happened to you. I want to listen to you. I want to help you see it wasn't your fault.

> Dear adult,
>
> There are so many incidents. I remember one time when my oldest brother came in and sat on my bed. I can remember him rubbing his tail (penis) on my privates and it felt nice. Later I felt so bad I wanted to run away. I couldn't bear to see him or anyone else because of the guilt, shame and fear that someone would find out what I'd done. But I used to egg him on. I wanted him to think I wanted it, even though I knew I would feel bad afterward. It was the only time he, or anyone else, was ever nice to me. It made me feel important. I liked the attention, so I was as bad as he was.

> Dear child,
>
> It was brave of you to tell me this. Don't feel bad because you let your older brother do sexual things with you or that you received some brief pleasure. He was older and should have known better. It was your way of surviving. If you had been loved and cuddled by your family, then this would probably not have happened.
>
> Write to me again and tell me how you are feeling.

> Dear adult,
>
> I feel so miserable I don't want to get out of bed. My brothers just tease me and won't let me play. I feel so alone. I'm so angry. My mom ignores me and my dad hits me all the time.

Dear child,

It's OK to be angry—it doesn't mean you don't care about your family. Your brothers were probably being mean to you because they felt bad about what they were doing to you and didn't want to be reminded of it. Your parents are also responsible for emotionally and physically abusing you—don't be ashamed. No one will abuse you now because I will take care of you. Hiding in bed won't take your feelings away, but talking will help you cope with them. You can keep on writing letters to me and I will try to help you.

Survivors' comments

I looked at a photo of myself as a child before I began, to help me "tune in" to the exercise. I felt like a child as I wrote my letter from my inner child. As an adult again, I felt compassion for the first time for the child instead of the hatred I'd always felt before. I cried. Then I became angry that I'd felt so bad about myself for years because of what someone else had done to me. I also felt guilt and shame for having had such strong negative feelings toward my child self. —Maya

I felt sadness, helplessness, affection, warmth and rejection. It was too painful to think about for too long. Me as a child is like a ghost. Writing the letters to my inner child helped me to get a little more in touch with my childhood self. It will take several attempts before I expect any progress to be made. —Danny

When I was writing to the inner child, I felt like I was her mother and the child was someone else. It was very hard to write to the inner child. I remembered how alone I felt as a child. It brought back a lot of feelings that I had put out of my mind. I coped by going for a walk, then came back to it. I needed support from a friend. —Lesley

When you have finished your letters, take care of yourself. First, make sure you are fully back in the present. Use the grounding exercises in chapter 4, such as Exercise 4.5 (reality orientation), if you still feel as if you are a child. You are working through this book because you had a distressing childhood, so it is natural to feel upset when you look back at how you felt then.

Caring for Yourself as a Child

We hope you now have more understanding of yourself as a child and can see how your childhood problems related to the pain and confusion you experienced. Now you may be able to give yourself some of the care and understanding you needed as a child.

EXERCISE 10.4
CARING FOR THE CHILD YOU WERE

Purpose   To help you understand and care more for the child you were.

- Find a photograph of yourself as a child. Look at the photograph and remember how you felt then. Think about what you would have liked from the adults around you. Keep this photograph with you, think of the child with sympathy and learn to accept the child. (If you do not have a photograph, you could use a childhood toy or possession to help you remember how you felt then.)
- Think of yourself as a child and sit for a moment with your feelings. Now try to see yourself as a child. Some people find it helps them to pick up a pillow or a soft toy and cuddle it. Imagine the pillow or toy is you as a child and see if you can give yourself some of the physical and emotional affection you needed as a child.
- Make notes here on anything that comes up for you.

_____

_____

_____

_____

_____

_____

_____

_____

_____

_____

Example

> When I thought of myself as a child, I remember playing with my dolls, brushing their long, beautiful hair. I would dress up in my mother's clothes and put on makeup. What I really wanted was to be cuddled before I went to bed. I wanted my mother to read me a story so I could fall asleep in her arms, and I wanted to play my music on my own tape deck. I just wanted to be loved. Now I can begin to give the child the love she needed. —Lesley

Survivor's comment

> I didn't have a photograph or very much left from my early childhood, so I imagined myself as a small child and I held an old teddy bear. I realized I used to give my teddy the hugs and talks I craved as a child. —Catherine

It can be helpful to do this exercise regularly to allow yourself to learn to care for the child you were and for you to give the child some of the love he or she needed.

You may have felt alone and not worth being cared for as a child, but that is not true now. Like many other survivors of childhood sexual abuse, you have taken the brave step of beginning to work on your problems and take care of yourself.

Now that you have begun the process of relating better to yourself as a child, it may be helpful to think about difficulties you may have now in relating to other children.

Difficulties Relating to Children

When someone was abused as a child or had a difficult childhood, he or she sometimes experiences difficulties in relating to children. The next exercise explores the range of difficulties survivors commonly experience with their own or other children.

EXERCISE 10.5 RELATING TO CHILDREN

Purpose   To look at the difficulties survivors of childhood sexual abuse experience with children.

Below is a list of difficulties survivors experience with children. Look through this list and check any that apply to you. You may be able to add other items to the list.

Difficulties with children

	Applies to you?		
	Yes	*No*	*Sometimes*
Excessive fears for children's safety	___	___	___
Overprotecting children	___	___	___
Inappropriately protecting children	___	___	___
Rejecting children	___	___	___
Anger and hostility toward children	___	___	___
Not being able to show love and affection toward children	___	___	___
Not being able to touch children	___	___	___
Controlling children	___	___	___
Having difficulties with children of a certain age	___	___	___
Not being able to bathe children	___	___	___
Having urges to abuse children	___	___	___
Physically abusing children	___	___	___
Emotionally abusing children	___	___	___
Sexually abusing children	___	___	___
Verbally abusing children	___	___	___
Overindulging children	___	___	___
Being jealous of children	___	___	___
Not being able to assert your own needs with children	___	___	___
Not being able to say "No" to children	___	___	___
Feeling helpless and out of control with children	___	___	___
Not feeling love for your own children	___	___	___
Excessively washing children	___	___	___
Unable to cope with a child feeling upset/hurt/angry	___	___	___
Confusing your own feelings with the child's	___	___	___
_____	___	___	___
_____	___	___	___
_____	___	___	___
_____	___	___	___
_____	___	___	___
_____	___	___	___
_____	___	___	___

If you have physically, sexually or emotionally abused children, or have urges to do so, it is important that you seek professional help for yourself and the children you have harmed as soon as possible. The services listed in the Resources section will be able to advise you.

Examples

Annabelle discovered she experienced several of the above difficulties and added the following:

> I didn't want to have children and was afraid of becoming pregnant.
> Despite that fear, I was reluctant to use contraception because I didn't want to acknowledge I was sexually active.
> I strongly preferred having a girl to having a boy.

Maya added

> Not having empathy with children.
> Not being in tune with children's needs.
> Behaving erratically and inconsistently with children.

Jenny added

> Being angry with them for being vulnerable or needy.
> Being unable to meet a child's needs/demands.

> **Survivor's comment**
>
> I feel embarrassed that I have such negative feelings for children in general. I coped by accepting that this is how I feel, although this is difficult to accept. I recognized that my feelings about children are because of my own unmet needs.   —Jenny

Why Do Survivors Have Difficulties with Children?

Survivors' Neediness

We have seen in this chapter how abused children often have no adult in their lives who understands how they are feeling, or no one to look after them and care about how they feel. As adults, survivors of childhood sexual abuse may still be needy themselves, and this can make it difficult for them to meet the needs and demands of their own children. Survivors may also try to compensate for their own neediness by giving their children everything they didn't have themselves, even if this is not what their children need or want. Some survivors feel jealous or resentful of children because the children are receiving love or other things they themselves were deprived of:

> I was jealous of my children having birthday parties and enjoying Christmas because I never enjoyed family activities like that.
> —Annabelle

You have now begun to give the child you were some understanding and care. This may help you relate to other children in terms of what they need rather than what you needed as a child.

Reminders of the Abuse

Survivors often cope with their childhood abuse by burying painful memories and feelings. Being with children can remind survivors of their own childhood and bring back the distressing feelings and memories they have pushed away. Working through this book may help you come to terms with your past so that being with children no longer triggers bad memories.

Lack of a Good Parenting Model

People usually learn the basic ideas of parenting from observing their own parents' behavior. Survivors who have been abused by their parents or other caregivers may have difficulty parenting because they have never learned the basic skills that others take for granted. You may find it helpful to share your anxieties or concerns with other parents, read a book on childcare, attend a parenting-skills class or talk to a social worker or a pediatric nurse at your child's doctor's office. Don't be afraid to ask for help or share your concerns with others.

In our book *Surviving Childhood Sexual Abuse* we discuss the difficulties survivors experience in relating to children—and how to overcome them—in more detail.

Looking back on your childhood problems and how you felt as a child can be painful, but beginning to understand and take care of yourself as a child can help you feel better about yourself now, and may also help you in your relationships with other children. It may help you put the past behind you and enable you to live your life in the present.

The next chapter helps you see how much progress you have made so far and helps you start to plan and look forward to your future.

PART 4

Looking toward the Future

This section helps you assess your progress so far and plan for a more positive future.

Past, Present and Future

11

> Doing these exercises has helped me see I have come a long way from when I first started working on the abuse. I have still got things in my life that I need to deal with but I intend to face them. —*Lesley*

This is the last chapter—congratulations on making it this far! It may have been difficult at times, and probably you will have experienced some very powerful emotions along the way. This chapter looks at how you have progressed in breaking free from your past and helps you assess your present position and make plans for your future. The chapter is divided into six sections:

- How have I changed?
- My progress
- Maintaining progress and dealing with relapses
- What I still want to do
- The next step
- How I feel now

How Have I Changed?

After working through this book, some survivors of childhood sexual abuse will have changed a lot, while others may feel they have not changed much at all. Each person makes changes at the right time and at the right pace for him or her. You may have changed in the way you think about your past and about yourself, but your feelings may take longer to change. Sometimes it can be hard to see the progress you have made:

> Ask others to tell you how far you have come if you can't remember. Other people can see changes in us that we don't—write down what they say and keep it. —*Rebecca*

219

The exercises in this section are intended to help you become aware of any changes you have made in your beliefs, feelings, symptoms, coping strategies and relationships.

Moving on and making progress does not mean overcoming all your problems; it does mean taking a few positive steps toward your future. It may mean you feel a little less guilty about the abuse, or that you binge and vomit less frequently. You may still feel depressed, but not all the time now or not quite as deeply as before. Everybody has times when they feel low or revert to old ways of thinking or behaving. It is common to have bad days, and on bad days everything seems to look worse than usual. To get a more realistic picture of how you have moved on, avoid working through this chapter on a bad day.

> When I tried these exercises the first time, I was having a bad day and I couldn't remember how I had changed. Don't do them when you are having an "off" day. Do the exercises in this chapter from a position of strength. Allow it to be the truth. —*Rebecca*

EXERCISE 11.1 HOW HAVE I CHANGED? BELIEFS ABOUT ABUSE

Purpose   To help you see whether you have made any changes in your beliefs about who is responsible for sexual abuse.

Look through the following list of beliefs and for each one ask yourself: "How much do I believe this right now?" Choose the number that corresponds with how much you believe each one. For example,

- If you don't believe the statement at all, circle 0.
- If you are unsure, circle 5.
- If you totally believe it, circle 10.

	Don't believe at all	*?*	*Totally believe*
I could not stop the abuse because the abuser had power over me	0 1 2 3 4	5 6	7 8 9 10
There are good reasons why I couldn't tell anyone	0 1 2 3 4	5 6	7 8 9 10

	Don't believe at all	?	Totally believe

I was abused because an abuser had access to me, not because of anything I had done   0 1 2 3 4 5 6 7 8 9 10

Abusers are always responsible for abusing children   0 1 2 3 4 5 6 7 8 9 10

I know my abuser was responsible for abusing me   0 1 2 3 4 5 6 7 8 9 10

The abuse was definitely not my fault   0 1 2 3 4 5 6 7 8 9 10

If you had more than one abuser:

I had more than one abuser because several abusers had access to me   0 1 2 3 4 5 6 7 8 9 10

I had more than one abuser because I was in a vulnerable and unprotected situation   0 1 2 3 4 5 6 7 8 9 10

When you have completed this exercise, you may want to compare your answers with those you gave in Exercise 5.2 to see if you changed any of your beliefs about abuse as you worked through this book. Every small step toward feeling less guilty is an important step forward.

> I believe I have gained power back from my abusers. The knowledge I have now makes me feel so strong. The more you recognize where the blame lies, the better you feel and the stronger you get.
> —Pauline

EXERCISE 11.2 HOW HAVE I CHANGED? FEELINGS ABOUT MYSELF

Purpose To rate the way you feel about yourself now.

Look through the following list of statements and circle the number that corresponds to how much you agree with each one. For example,

- If you totally agree with the statement, circle 0.
- If you neither agree nor disagree, circle 5.
- If you totally disagree, circle 10.

Feelings about myself	*Agree*					*?*			*Disagree*		
I hate myself	0	1	2	3	4	5	6	7	8	9	10
I don't like myself	0	1	2	3	4	5	6	7	8	9	10
I feel worthless	0	1	2	3	4	5	6	7	8	9	10
I don't accept myself	0	1	2	3	4	5	6	7	8	9	10
I am bad	0	1	2	3	4	5	6	7	8	9	10
I do not like the child I was	0	1	2	3	4	5	6	7	8	9	10
I do not feel positive about the future	0	1	2	3	4	5	6	7	8	9	10
I feel helpless	0	1	2	3	4	5	6	7	8	9	10

EXERCISE 11.3 HOW HAVE I CHANGED? MY RELATIONSHIP WITH MY FEELINGS

Purpose   To look at how you relate to your feelings now.

Look through the following list of statements and circle the number that corresponds to how much you agree with each one. For example,

- If you totally agree with the statement, circle 0.
- If you neither agree nor disagree, circle 5.
- If you totally disagree, circle 10.

My Feelings	*Agree*					*?*			*Disagree*		
I am overwhelmed by my feelings	0	1	2	3	4	5	6	7	8	9	10
I am not in touch with my feelings	0	1	2	3	4	5	6	7	8	9	10
I am frightened of my own feelings	0	1	2	3	4	5	6	7	8	9	10

I am cut off from my feelings	0	1	2	3	4	5	6	7	8	9	10
I am ill at ease with my feelings	0	1	2	3	4	5	6	7	8	9	10

You may want to compare your ratings now with how you answered the same exercises (2.2 and 2.3) earlier in the book. See if you feel a little better about yourself now or feel more comfortable with your own feelings.

EXERCISE 11.4   HOW HAVE I CHANGED? SYMPTOMS AND COPING STRATEGIES

Purpose   To help you notice if your symptoms are lessening, or any positive changes in your use of coping strategies.

Think back to the symptoms you had and the harmful coping strategies you used before you started working on the abuse. Help yourself become aware of any reductions in your symptoms or changes in your use of coping strategies by writing them down under the headings below. *Rebecca's answers to this exercise have been written underneath each one as examples.*

- **Symptoms or harmful coping strategies I no longer have:**
  I don't self-injure any more.

  _____

  _____

  _____

  _____

  _____

- **Symptoms or harmful coping strategies that happen less often:**
  I occasionally have flashbacks, nightmares and hallucinations and I still isolate myself sometimes. I don't use illness as often to escape problems.

  _____

  _____

  _____

  _____

  _____

- **Symptoms I can cope with now:**
  I still hear negative messages in my head from the people who abused me and the people who should have taken care of me, but I am not as afraid of them. Blocking out feelings is less of a problem, and I can stay in a situation now even if it's uncomfortable. I still get frightened, but now I can talk about my feelings.

  _____

  _____

  _____

  _____

  _____

- **Symptoms and harmful coping strategies I still need to work on:**
  The things I need to work on are binge-eating, fear of sexual and nonsexual relationships and my fear of being humiliated.

  _____

  _____

  _____

  _____

  _____

Examples

Lesley

- **Symptoms or harmful coping strategies I no longer have:**
  I don't take drugs and I don't drink too much now. I don't make myself sick or hurt myself anymore.

- **Symptoms or harmful coping strategies that happen less often:**
  I still have nightmares and flashbacks occasionally and become afraid of closing the bedroom door. I can cope with dark places more often now.

- **Symptoms I can cope with now:**
  I still see my abuser's face sometimes when I'm having sex but I can cope with it more easily. I'm getting better at going places where there are a lot of people.

- **Symptoms and harmful coping strategies I still need to work on:**
  I still cope at difficult times by not eating and I still look around when I'm out to see if my abusers are there. I love my kids and I need to work on showing I love them and I really want to be able to say it to them.

Maya
- **Symptoms or harmful coping strategies I no longer have:**
  I don't try to "fix" other people. I don't smoke.

- **Symptoms or harmful coping strategies that happen less often:**
  I'm not as obsessed with exercising. I still have problems with food (binge/starve cycle), depression and "spacing out," but they don't last as long as they used to.

- **Symptoms I can cope with now:**
  I'm not as frightened of people's anger, and I don't feel as guilty for telling about my abuse.

- **Symptoms and harmful coping strategies I still need to work on:**
  I still burn myself, take too many tranquilizers or drink too much alcohol when things go wrong. I am still defensive and overcontrolling.

> The exercise made me realize how far I've come, but I was also scared when I saw how many symptoms I still had to work on. However, it has also made me more determined to succeed. Keep on trying—you will succeed in the end, and so will I.   —Pauline

EXERCISE 11.5
HOW HAVE I CHANGED? RELATIONSHIPS

Purpose   To check for improvements in your relationships with people and to look at which changes you still want to work on.

Think about your relationships with friends, family, sexual partners, children, work colleagues or others. Have they changed in any way? Make some notes below on any improvements in your relationships, however small, and any problems you still need to work on. *Rebecca's answers to the exercise are given as examples.*

It was easier for me to do the exercise by splitting it into different categories like family, friends, work colleagues and sexual relationships and thinking about each separately. —Rebecca

- **Positive changes in my relationships:**
  I relate to my family on equal terms now and I have started to relate to children. My friendships are more equal and are deeper. They are now based on mutual support, not what they can give me. I also have more positive relationships at work.

  _____

  _____

  _____

  _____

  _____

- **Relationship problems I still need to work on:**
  I still react resentfully when my mother asks me to do things, especially when she uses manipulation and the "poor me" trip. I need to be more assertive with people. I still need to do a lot of work on relationships that are potentially sexual.

  _____

  _____

  _____

  _____

  _____

Examples

Anthony

Positive changes in my relationships:
I can talk openly to the family about the abuse and I don't fly off the handle when the abuser's name is mentioned. Now I know I have some very good friends who know I have been abused and will listen to me when I get down in the dumps.

Relationship problems I still need to work on:
I still get angry with people and I have to work on my temper, which I lose sometimes. Sometimes when I'm out with my friends it's hard for

me to be with people, and I just take off. I know they worry about me.
That's when self-harm might happen—when I'm on my own like that.

Pauline
Positive changes in my relationships:
  Now I feel more equal with my partner. I do not take my feelings out
  on my child.
Relationship problems I still need to work on:
  I still give in to what other people want.

> This exercise made me happy because it helped me see that there
> *are* positive developments in my current relationships. It also gave me
> a focus for other areas to improve. —*Rebecca*

The betrayal involved in sexual abuse often creates problems in some or
all of the survivor's later relationships. Be aware of any small
improvements you have made in your relationships and remember you
can continue to work on making your relationships better. After doing the
exercises in this book, you may feel better about yourself and have
worked through your feelings about other people. Making these changes
in yourself can help in your relationships with others but sometimes it is
necessary to work with a therapist to improve your relationships. If you
still have serious problems in your relationships, you may want to think
about seeking individual or group therapy.

The first four exercises were intended to help you see any progress
you have made in the way you think and feel, in your symptoms and
ways of coping, and in your relationships:

> Looking back at the way my life was, I can see the progress I've made
> now. —*Catherine*

There will almost certainly be areas you still need to work on—
self-development is a lifelong task. For now, try to focus on the positive
changes you have made; later in the chapter we will take a look at issues
you may still need to work on.

My Progress

> Looking at the ways I have improved made me feel excited and gave
> me a sense of achievement. —*Rebecca*

The next exercise is meant to help you pull together the changes you have made in different parts of your life and celebrate any progress you have made so far. Representing your journey to healing in some way can help you see where you have come from, where you are now, and increase your awareness of the changes you have made.

Children have to use all the resources available to them to find ways of living through the trauma of sexual abuse and of keeping some part of themselves safe. Finding ways of surviving sexual abuse is a creative process. Many survivors produce imaginative writing, poetry and artwork. You may enjoy using your creativity to represent your journey toward healing and to celebrate your progress.

EXERCISE 11.6   MY PROGRESS

Purpose   To represent and celebrate your journey toward breaking free from the effects of childhood sexual abuse.

Represent the changes you have made so far in one of the ways suggested below. This exercise is *not* about what you still have to do but is a way of focusing on the positive steps you have made already and celebrating your courage and success. Choose the way that suits you and enjoy yourself.

- Draw or paint yourself and your life at the beginning of your journey to healing and where you are now.

Or

- Draw a cartoon strip showing the stages you have been through.

Or

- Represent your journey through poetry, music or dance.

Or

- Write about any positive changes you are aware of in yourself or your life since you started working on the abuse. You could write about how you overcame difficulties you faced and about any changes in the way you feel about yourself. What do you enjoy now about yourself and your life?

My Progress

Examples

Maya

    Striding out
    Purposefully,
    Strong and upright
    Along the path of freedom.
    Treading softly,
    Tentatively,
    Feeling my way forward.
    Leaping, sprinting,
    Scaling great heights.
    Trudging wearily,
    Stumbling, falling,
    Finding a shoulder
    To lean on
    Until refreshed.
    I start again,
    Unfettered.
    Experiencing life anew.
    Reborn
    After therapy.

Pauline

Pauline created this way of representing the stages she has moved through:

> I chose a bunch of different outfits from my wardrobe and I taped some songs. I started by sitting in the corner crying like a lost orphan, and I played *Amazing Grace*. I continued by changing my clothes and changing my image as I played different songs. As I went along, I felt stronger and more positive until I ended up wearing a red dress with my hair piled up, high-heeled shoes on and a red handbag. I felt so powerful, and I played *Simply the Best*.
>
> I felt emotional expressing the stages I have gone through, right up to when I felt very strong and powerful. It really helped me get things out of my system. Everyone has to find the way that suits them, but this worked wonders for me!

Maintaining Progress and Dealing with Relapses

> Becoming aware of the changes I have made scared me at first—knowing that although I have moved on, a lot things could still backtrack.   —Rebecca

Looking at your progress may give you a sense of achievement, but it can also make you afraid of slipping back to how you were. At certain times you may find it hard to cope. It is normal to have good and bad days. You may become distressed by situations that remind you of your abuse, or you may be suffering from the normal stresses of life. At these times, distressing feelings from the past can return and you may revert to old, harmful coping methods. This can make you think you have gone back to the beginning instead of realizing that you are having a temporary setback. The next exercise asks you to produce a list of nonharmful coping strategies for use during difficult times.

EXERCISE 11.7 POSITIVE COPING STRATEGIES I USE NOW

Purpose   To have a list of nonharmful coping strategies ready to use when you are feeling bad.

By now, you may have replaced some of your harmful coping strategies with more nonharmful ones. Write a list here of the positive ways you now use to cope when you are under stress or feeling bad.

Positive coping strategies

_____

_____

_____

_____

_____

_____

_____

_____

_____

_____

Examples

Lesley

Keep my mind busy.
Get out of the house.
Talk to others.
Go for a walk or a drive.
Clean out a cupboard.
Do something positive.
Have a good cry.
Deal with my problems a little at a time.

Rebecca

Now when I'm having difficulties, I
Ask for help.
Write things down.
Challenge negative self-talk.
Seek out friends instead of spending all my time alone. Draw my
    feelings.
Do a sculpture of my feelings.
Write down, draw or sculpt nightmares and hallucinations.
Go out, maybe run errands instead of giving in to depression.
Work through them rather than let them destroy me.

Anthony

Writing letters to my abuser (not to send) to express my feelings.
Helping people and listening to other people's problems helps me realize
    I am not alone.
Keeping busy.
If I'm feeling really bad, I'll phone a helpline.
Talking to my close friends.

Pauline

    I challenge my negative thinking and try to remember everything I've
learned. I try to put it into practice. Sometimes it helps to sit and cry.

Maya

    If I have a bad day, I don't panic as much now, and I tell myself
everyone has bad days at times. Instead of avoiding my problems, I am
more likely to face them by writing them down, expressing my feelings
and taking action rather than giving in and feeling helpless. This helps
me control my mood swings. I don't get as high these days, and my lows
don't last as long. My dog is a very positive influence on me. I hug her,
kiss her, stroke her, cry on her and she doesn't mind at all. She needs a
lot of exercise, so I have something to get out of bed for, and the walks
are good for me.

Your positive coping strategies may help you overcome your difficulties,
but sometimes you may continue to feel bad or have symptoms return for a
longer period. The next exercise suggests ways of dealing with relapses. It is
much more difficult to think of positive things when you are feeling bad, so
spend some time now, or when you are in a positive mood, thinking of
what you can do to help yourself if you do go through a difficult period.

> It is important that you do this exercise when you are feeling positive,
> so all your helpful suggestions are ready for you when you feel down.
> —Rebecca

EXERCISE 11.8
POSITIVE WAYS OF DEALING WITH RELAPSES

Purpose　To look at ways of dealing with relapses and continuing the
progress you have made.
  Read through the list below of positive ways of dealing with relapses
and add others if you think of them.

Positive Ways to Deal with Relapses

- Tell myself it's normal to have relapses now and then, and that I can get through it.
- Remember I've felt this bad before and it will pass.
- Take one day at a time.
- Remind myself that I have made progress and that this is a temporary setback—I am *not* back at the beginning.
- Write down how I feel.
- Try to use my positive coping strategies—see list in Exercise 11.7, above.
- Go through chapters 3 and 4 on coping strategies and dealing with symptoms again.
- Talk to a friend.
- Contact one of the people on my list from Exercise 1.1.
- Work through this book again.
- Contact my primary-care doctor.
- Phone a telephone helpline.
- Get some professional support or therapy.
- Think about how far I've come and how I'm going to persevere with the journey.

_____

_____

_____

_____

_____

_____

_____

Remember: You are not alone! Asking for help is a positive coping strategy.

Example

Calli

- I think of the positive changes that have happened.
- I pray.
- I say self-affirmations like, "You are doing well."
- I contact friends.
- I treat myself to something I want, like a music CD.

Some weeks I can feel really bad and even feel like I'm slipping, but then I remember how far I've come and things turn around soon. I decided my abuser wasn't going to win. With that thought, I can wade through the bad stuff.   —*Anita B.*

I coped with my fear of everything going wrong by writing down all my positive coping strategies and remembering all the useful contacts and support I have now. I also know that I've pulled myself together before, so I can do it again.   —*Rebecca*

It helps to know it's natural to relapse, so you don't feel like a failure when it happens. I did relapse and I was terrified. I thought everything was happening all over again and I'd never get out of it. I got some help and now I'm a lot better again.   —*Pauline*

If you begin to feel distressed or down, turn to these exercises. Remind yourself of the nonharmful coping strategies you can use and the things that can help you cope with relapses.

What I Still Want to Do

Now may be a good time to think about what you still want to do and what kind of a person you would like to be when you have overcome the constraints imposed by your past. You will probably still need to work on issues and problems resulting from the abuse and still want to make changes in yourself and your life. When you were a child, the adults around you may have had expectations of how they wanted you to be, or told you how you were going to turn out, but now try to think about how *you* would like to be in the future.

EXERCISE 11.9 WHAT I STILL WANT TO DO

Purpose   To look at what you still want to achieve on your journey toward breaking free of the past.
   Spend some time thinking about any changes you still want to make in

- The way you live
- Your interests/hobbies
- Your job/occupation/career
- Qualifications or skills
- The way you look

- Your marriage, partnership, sexual relationships or love life
- Your friendships or other relationships
- The kind of person you are (personality, strengths, attributes, personal style)

Also think about

- What you still want to do
- Problems you still need to solve

What I still want to do

Here are suggestions for representing what you still want to do and how you would like to be in the future. Try all of them, or choose the one that suits you.

- Write a description of your future self using the list above to help you. You may find it easier to write in the third person rather than using "I." For example: "Amanda is a strong person. She is kind to other people but she also knows how to take care of herself."
- Make a drawing or a cartoon strip of the life you would like to lead and how you would like to be.
- Fill in the shapes on the next page.

Use this space to write a description of the person you would like to be, or make a drawing.

Fill in the shapes with the things you still want to change in your life. (See example below.)

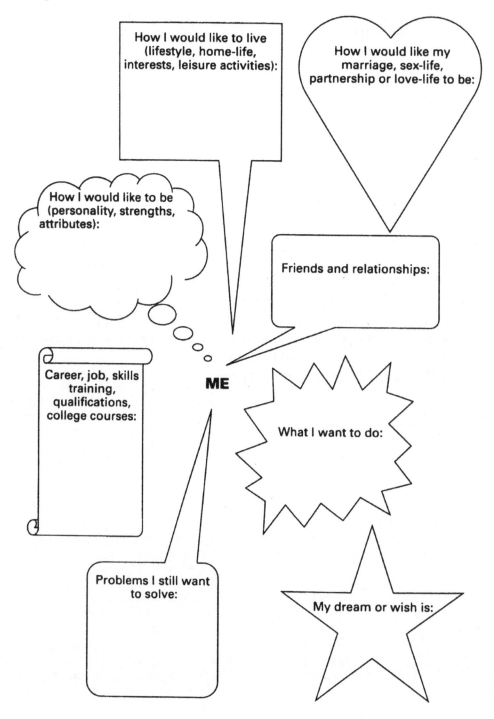

How I would like to live (lifestyle, home-life, interests, leisure activities):

How I would like my marriage, sex-life, partnership or love-life to be:

How I would like to be (personality, strengths, attributes):

Friends and relationships:

Career, job, skills training, qualifications, college courses:

ME

What I want to do:

Problems I still want to solve:

My dream or wish is:

Example

How I would like to live (lifestyle, home-life, interests, leisure activities): *To own my own home and feel safe and secure, to try new activities like sculpture and ballroom dancing, to be more adventurous.*

How I would like my marriage, sex-life, partnership or love-life to be: *I'd like to feel able to have a loving, fulfilling sexual relationship.*

How I would like to be (personality, strengths, attributes): *I'd like to have higher self-esteem and a less negative attitude and to be less judgemental and more encouraging of others.*

Friends and relationships: *To be able to maintain deeper relationships.*

REBECCA

Career, job, skills training, qualifications, college courses: To change my job to something other than a care worker. To earn a degree and get my teaching certificate.

What I want to do: *I just want to be content.*

Problems I still want to solve: *Eating problem, weight problem, lack of a relationship. To look after myself better by resting and not overworking.*

My dream or wish is: *To have a family*

I would like to be able to live my life without getting angry whenever abuse is talked about on the news or other TV programs. I want to be able to show my love to my three children and wife and let them know how much I appreciate them. I wish I could enjoy sex with my wife without getting uptight and having my mind full of thoughts I can't get rid of. I don't want all the frills of life, I just want to be a normal happy father and husband.   —*Graham*

I would like to be strong in myself and to say "No" and mean it. I would like to be more patient and not so quick-tempered. I want to feel a lot better about myself and have a better dress sense, and I'd like to weigh about 140 pounds.   —*Paula*

I would like to overcome my nervousness and anxiety and have more freedom from family commitments. I like to socialize with my caring friends, which is rewarding for me, and I want to develop my interest in breeding budgies and cockatiels.   —*Anthony*

Comments about the exercise

It was hard to start this exercise because it's hard for me to say "I want." It brings up old fears—saying "I want" usually means you can't have it or someone will take it away. Saying "I want" means being assertive and positive. I'm going to use "I want" from now on. This exercise was helpful to me because I knew I wanted to be different, but I didn't have any idea about who I wanted to be. It gave me hope, and it was hard for me to stop doing this exercise! It's important to be as realistic as possible and not aim to be Superperson.   —*Rebecca*

I've avoided some problems up to now. I know I have to deal with them, but I am not sure how to at this point. Having looked back to where I was—I never thought I would be the way I am now. Who knows how much further I can go?   —*Anita B.*

EXERCISE 11.10
BEING MY FUTURE SELF

Purpose   To see how it feels to be the person you want to be.

Imagine you are now the person you described in the previous exercise. Sit or stand as he or she would. Try to feel as this person would feel (for example, confident, content, determined) for five minutes. Practice being your future self for a short time each day. After you have practiced for a while, you may want to try being this "new you" for longer periods.

> I have tried being this kind of person and I do feel a lot better about myself. When I try to be my ideal self, I always sit up straight. I seem to laugh more and feel more confident. —*Paula*

> A good self-reflective exercise to do whether you have been abused or not. This shows a positive approach to the future, and makes me feel more self-confident and in control if I take a chance. —*Catherine*

EXERCISE 11.11
MAKING CHANGES

Purpose   To help you plan for the changes you want to make in your life.

1) Look back at Exercise 11.9 and think of two or three things you would like to change about yourself or your life. Choose the easiest ones first. It is important that you choose small changes that you are able to do now. For example:

- Change your hairstyle.
- Ask people to call you Amanda instead of Mandy.
- Join an assertiveness-training class.
- Get exercise.
- Register for a class.
- Buy clothes to suit the "new" you.
- Try to feel better about yourself by continuing to work through this book or do something for yourself every day.

Write them here.

I would like to
(for example, "I would like to learn to cook better.")

-
-
-

2) Think of ways of achieving each goal. Write down how you will do it.

I will do it by
(for example, "I could sign up for an evening cooking class.")

-
-
-

    3) What is stopping you from making these changes?

(for example, "I'm scared of going to the adult learning center.")

-
-
-

    4) How can you overcome these obstacles?

(for example, "I could ask a friend to go with me.")

-
-
-

Why not start now? If you can't start immediately, pick a date when you will begin to make these changes in your life.

When you have achieved these changes, you may want to think of taking three more small steps.

Examples
Paula

I would like to

- Lose weight.
- Control my temper.
- Change my dress sense.

I will do it by

- I am on a diet to lose weight.
- I sit in a room by myself to control my temper.
- I have started to buy and wear bright-looking clothes.

Anita B.

I would like to

- Become more assertive.
- Become qualified in some area.
- Believe in myself.

I will do it by

- Taking an assertiveness-training class.
- Enrolling in college.
- Hopefully by doing both of the above I will learn to believe in myself.

These exercises were very helpful to me and I think it's a good idea to go back to them at different stages of the healing process. I needed to focus on what was stopping me from becoming the person I wanted to be. I realized I unconsciously needed to be a victim (as an adult) because I was too scared to be anything else—it was all I'd ever known.   —*Sarah*

I never dared to look at what the future could hold before.   —*Anita B.*

Doing the exercises in this chapter made me realize how much the abuse has affected me. It was hard to look deep into myself, and I had a lot of mixed feelings about where I am now and where I would like to be. It was also difficult to realize I have to make changes in myself in order to feel happy. By doing these exercises you *can* begin to make changes in your life.   —*Lesley*

In the past, other people controlled your life and your feelings. Thinking of a positive future for yourself and taking even tiny steps toward it can make you feel more in control of your own life. Keep returning to these exercises and plan a few more small steps forward. Step by step you can walk toward the life you want to have, even though it may take you over a long and difficult path. Try to see there is a light at the end of the tunnel, and head toward it.

The Next Step

The purpose of this book is to help you begin the process of working through your problems and accepting yourself more, so you can move on through your life free of the past's shadow. The important thing is that *you have started the process*, not whether you have made big or small steps forward. Try not to compare your progress with that of the survivors of childhood sexual abuse who have contributed examples and quotations to this book.

Some of you will feel you have worked on your abuse enough, at least for now, and have achieved as much as you want to at this point. You may understand more about what happened to you and who was really responsible for the abuse. You may now want to put the abuse behind you and continue creating your own future. Some of you may wish to join awareness or support groups for survivors of childhood sexual abuse. Some survivors become activists against childhood sexual abuse, but remember it is important to be clear about your own feelings and problems before you try to help other people.

> Doing these exercises brought up a lot of things for me. I feel very mixed up right now. I have come a long way, but I still have a long way to go. Before I was in a tunnel with no light. Now I'm beginning to see a little light. I have to come to terms with a lot of things that, before doing these exercises, I could put at the back of my mind. I want therapy again, because there are things I want to talk about and I want to deal with for my own sake as well as my family's.   —*Lesley*

Like Lesley, many of you will have found that working through this book has stirred up thoughts and feelings that you still need to work on. You may want to do this by continuing to work on the exercises in this book or by continuing with therapy you are currently involved with. You may feel you are now ready to go for some individual or group therapy; asking for therapy may be difficult, but it can also be the way to receive the help you deserve.

> I was frightened by the idea of therapy. It was the thought of other people knowing I was abused. I was also scared of not being believed. I told someone and I was believed, and that was my first step ahead. Now I don't care who knows that I have been abused. I am not ashamed. I didn't do anything wrong.   —*Lesley*

The last exercise asks you to take time to think about what you want to do next. It is not about what you *should* do, but about what is the right thing for you to do.

EXERCISE 11.12 THE NEXT STEP

Purpose To help you think about what you will do next.

Now that you have nearly finished this book, it is time to think about what you want to do next. Read the following list and check any of the items that seem right for you.

What do you want to do now?	Applies to you?
Take a well-earned break	_____
Take a break, then continue working on my problems	_____
Get some therapy or professional help	_____
Continue with therapy	_____
Join a survivors' group	_____
Continue to work through this workbook	_____
Take an assertiveness-training or confidence-building class	_____
Move on with life	_____
Continue to develop my potential	_____
Meet or network with other survivors	_____
Campaign for awareness of childhood abuse and for resources for survivors of childhood sexual abuse	_____
Celebrate my progress	_____

Write down anything else you would like to do now:

_____

_____

_____

_____

_____

_____

_____

_____

_____

(continued)

Write down the steps you can take to achieve this:

_____

_____

_____

_____

_____

_____

_____

_____

Examples

Pauline

I want to

Take a well-earned break.

Move on with my life and put the abuse behind me.

Continue to develop my potential.

Network with other survivors.

I will do this by

Taking a course in interior design.

Attend a local support group for survivors.

Maya

I want to

Relax—chill out and take life as it comes.

I will do this by

Having fun, riding my bike, painting, playing with the dog, jumping in puddles, flying a kite, taking some kids out. Sitting in the garden on my lounger and lounging. Trying aromatherapy. Going out and sharing a laugh with friends. Having sex in the shower (with my husband)!

Calli

I want to

Take another vacation.

Make some new friends.

Write a book.
Realize the wealth of potential within.
Live life to the fullest.
I will do this by
Taking all opportunities as they arise.

> This exercise made me a little fearful about the future. It really helped me to acknowledge my feelings of fear about the future and also my fear of letting go of the past and moving on.   —*Rebecca*

It takes courage to read this book, look back on a painful part of your life and work through the distressing feelings and problems that often result from childhood abuse. We hope you have made some progress in breaking free from your past and that you now have hopes and dreams for the future. Society still has a long way to go in providing help for child and adult survivors of childhood sexual abuse, providing treatment for abusers and changing the legal system to be more responsive to child abuse issues. Society is, however, at last facing up to the reality and scale of child abuse. Perhaps we can celebrate the progress we have made as a society and as individuals in recognizing child abuse and acknowledging and helping its victims.

> Keep on moving ahead!   —*Rebecca*

How I Feel Now

It seems fitting to end this book with some words of encouragement from survivors of childhood sexual abuse. Some of them are at the beginning of their personal journey, while others are receiving or have completed individual or group therapy as well as completing the exercises in this book. We asked them to write about "How I feel now."

Anita B. was raped by a family friend starting when she was eight years old.

> The exercises made me think about things I would have preferred to leave alone. At the time, it stirred up all kinds of emotions and I felt worse than when I started. But I stuck with it, and it did get better. Actually seeing my thoughts and feelings on paper seemed to put things in perspective. I feel much better now than I did. My confidence and self-esteem are higher than I've ever known. My life is entirely

different now. I see things clearly and I stand up for myself (something I've never done). Before, if anything went wrong, I would think it was my fault, but not any more. I feel like I'm a "real" person now, not just a front for others to see.

Pauline was sexually, physically and emotionally abused by many individuals, both inside and outside of her family.

I was too shy and scared to go for therapy in case they thought I was insane and locked me up. But I found the courage and went. Now I feel great. Most of the time I can be myself and be what I've always wanted to be.

Danny was physically and emotionally abused in his childhood by his parents and while in foster care.

I feel stronger within. I feel like I'm on the road to recovery. I also feel it is possible to combine the two extreme sides of myself to make a more interesting whole. I'm more positive, less aggressive and use my brain more. It's too early to tell where it will lead. It's getting better by degrees, but it can require a lot of mental effort. On a good day, I feel optimistic about the future because I like myself more than I used to. There are more good days now. It's still hard to fight back from a bad day, but the less booze I drink, the easier it is.

Jean was sexually abused by her father.

I'm beginning to accept that the abuse was not my fault and that I could not have prevented what happened. I am now releasing all the pent-up emotions I kept at bay most of my life: the guilt of blaming myself, feeling dirty. It's helped to find out that I'm not going insane because I was talking to people that only I could see. I'm beginning to see that there could be a light at the end of the tunnel. I'm determined to finally free myself of my abuser.

Catherine was sexually abused by her father.

Before, I didn't know if I lived in my mind or my body. Now I feel free, light and optimistic but, most important, I feel like me. Going through a bad life experience has turned me into a good person. Now I feel equal to most people. I like myself. I enjoy friendships. I see lots ahead.

Graham was sexually abused by his mother and her friends.

> I am not near the end of therapy yet, but I think it's working. I feel a lot better having someone to talk to. I do have bad days, but I think I'm coping and getting along.

Sarah was neglected and physically abused by her family and was also sexually abused both within and outside her family. She finished therapy some time ago and is now a counselor herself.

> I am stronger and in touch with reality now. I understand myself and my emotions much more. When I look back to who I was and who I have become, I feel proud. It's been hard work but worthwhile. I believe I could survive almost anything now. I feel so different. I wouldn't say I am fully healed, because that would mean I was perfect, and I want to continue exploring my *self*. It is strange sometimes when I hear my own clients and remember I once felt the way they do. I feel good knowing how far I have come. No longer a victim or a survivor, I'm me.

Calli was abused by an organized group of people, including her own family.

> I feel a sense of achievement. I no longer want to look back on my abuse. I prefer to look forward to the changes within that are enabling me to function as a human being. I believe I can live and enjoy life—I have confidence in me.

We admire your courage and wish you well.

Further Reading

Self-Help Books for Survivors

Ainscough, Carolyn, and Kay Toon. *Surviving Childhood Sexual Abuse: Revised edition.* Tucson, AZ: Fisher Books, 2000.

Allender, Dan B. *The Wounded Heart: Hope for adult victims of childhood sexual abuse.* Colorado Springs, CO: NavPress, 1990.

Bass, Ellen, and Laura Davis. *The Courage to Heal: A guide for women survivors of child sexual abuse, third edition.* New York: HarperPerennial Library, 1994.

Gannon, J. Patrick. *Soul Survivors: A new beginning for adults abused as children.* San Francisco, CA: Publishers Group West, 1999.

Gil, Eliana. *Outgrowing the Pain: A book for and about adults abused as children.* Rockville, MD: Launch, 1983.

Sanford, Linda T. *Strong at the Broken Places: Overcoming the trauma of childhood abuse.* New York: Avon Books, 1992.

For Survivors Abused by Women

Elliott, Michele (editor). *Female Sexual Abuse of Children: The ultimate taboo.* New York: Guilford Press, 1994.

For Male Survivors

Etherington, Kim. *Adult Male Survivors of Sexual Abuse.* Alexandria, VA: Pitman Publishing, 1995.

Grubman-Black, S. D. *Broken Boys, Mending Men: Recovery from childhood sexual abuse.* Blue Ridge Summit, PA: Tab Books, 1990.

Hunter, Mic. *Abused Boys: The neglected victims of sexual abuse.* Westminster, MD: Fawcett Books, 1991.

Lew, Mike, and Ellen Bass. *Victims No Longer: Men recovering from incest and other sexual child abuse.* New York: HarperCollins, 2000.

Autobiography

Angelou, Maya. *I Know Why the Caged Bird Sings.* New York: Bantam Books, 1983.

Fiction

Walker, Alice. *The Color Purple.* New York: Pocket Books, 1996.

For Partners and Families of Survivors

Davis, Laura. *Allies in Healing: When the person you love was sexually abused as a child.* New York: Harper Perennial, 2000.

Graber, Ken. *Ghosts in the Bedroom: A guide for partners of incest survivors.* Deerfield Park, FL: Health Communication, 1988.

For Therapists

Etherington, Kim. *Narrative Approaches to Working with Adult Male Survivors of Sexual Abuse: The clients', the counselor's and the researcher's stories.* London, England: Jessica Kingsley, 2000.

Hall, Liz, and Siobhan Lloyd. *Surviving Sexual Abuse: A handbook for helping women challenge their past, 2nd edition.* Falmer Press, 1989.

Books Referred to in the Text

Finkelhor, David. *Sexually Victimized Children: New theory and research.* New York: Free Press, 1981.

_____ and Sharon Araji. *A Sourcebook on Child Sexual Abuse.* Newbury Park, CA: Sage Publications, 1986.

Resources

A primary-care physician, social worker or other professional can assist you in getting help from a clinical psychologist or other therapist. Do not be afraid to ask to see a woman if you feel uncomfortable talking to a man (or vice versa).

The national addresses or phone numbers for various organizations are listed below. For information on local sources of help, contact the national office or try your local telephone directory. Please include a stamped, self-addressed envelope to these organizations if you want a written reply.

General Resources and Organizations

Association for the Treatment of Sexual Abusers
10700 SW Beaverton Hillsdale Hwy.
No. 26
Beaverton, OR 97005–3035
(503) 643–1023
http://www.atsa.com

Incest Survivors Anonymous
P.O. Box 17245
Long Beach, CA 90807–7245
(562) 428–5599

**International Society for the Prevention of
 Child Abuse and Neglect**
401 N. Michigan Ave., Suite 2200
Chicago, IL 60611
(312) 578–1401

Prevent Child Abuse America
P.O. Box 2866
Chicago, IL 60609
(312) 663–3520

Helplines

Girls and Boys Town
(800) 448–3000
http://www.boystown.org

Childhelp USA & Canada
(800) 422–4453

MensNet
http://www.magi.com/~mensnet/netsite.htm

National Child Abuse Hotline
http://www.childhelpusa.org

National Directory of Hotlines and
Crisis Intervention Centers' Covenant House Nineline
(800) 999–9999 (24-hour hotline for runaways and their families)

Rape, Abuse & Incest National Network
(800) 656–4673

Male Survivors

Male Abuse Survivors Support Forum
http://www.angelfire.com/nc/asarian/frames.hmtl

National Organization on Male Sexual Victimization
P.O. Box 20782
West Palm Beach, FL 33416
(800) 738–4181
http://www.nomsv.org

Internet Resources

Usenet groups
alt.support.abuse-partners
alt.sexual.abuse.recovery
alt.sexual.abuse.recovery.d

Web sites
Abuse/Incest support:
http://www.worldchat.com/public/asarc

Partners and allies of sexual assault survivors resources list:
http://idealist.com/wounded_healer/allies.shtml

POSitive Partners of Survivors (chat room):
http://clubs.yahoo.com/positivepartnersofsurvivors

Index

Normalization, behavior, 117, 118
Numbness, 34

O

Obsessive behavior, 30, 200
Obsessive-compulsive behavior, 144
Overachievement, 200
Overeating, 49, 53, 55, 199. *See also* Eating
    disorders
Overprotectiveness, 41
    toward mothers, 181

P

Painting, 11–12, 46–47, 49, 52, 55
    and emotional growth, 228
    and mothers, relationships with, 178
Panic attacks, 6, 40, 144
Parenting model
    lack of, 215
Passing out, 48
Pausing, 57
Pedophile groups, 117
Perfection, 199
Phobias, 30, 40, 200
Phoning, 49, 53, 55, 56
Physical abuse, 2
    awareness of, public, 108
Physical size
    of abusers, 96–100
    and power, 140–143
    of victims, 96–100
Physical strength
    of abusers, 93
Playing, 57
Poetry, 10
    and emotional growth, 228, 229
Police
    informing, of abuse, 143
Pornography, child, 117
Power
    and abuser, criminal activity of, 143–144
    of abusers, 93–96, 100
    emotional, 100
    and physical size, 140–143
Powerlessness, 30, 35, 39–40, 220
    and abusers, multiple, 137
    fear of, and guilt, 131–132, 139–144
    and flashbacks, 78–79
    and hallucinations, 78–79
Processing strategies, 46–47

Professional help, 2, 18, 146, 243
Professional workers, 19
Protection, 38
    lack of, 33
Protectors, 171, 221
    mothers as, 181–195

R

Rashes, 200
Reactions, abuser's
    and confrontations, 159–160
Reactions, mothers'
    to disclosure, 188–190
Reactions, people's
    and assertiveness, 167–168
    fear of, 7, 37, 103, 108–109
Reading, 49
Reality orientation, 79–80
Recovery
    methods of, 9–12
Red herrings, 168
    by abuser, 159, 161–162
Relapses, 230, 232–234
Relationship
    personal, and self-feelings, 34
Relationships
    with children, 212–215
    improvement in, and emotional growth,
        225–227
    later, and betrayal, 227
    problems with, 31
Resistance, child's
    and abusers, multiple, 137
    abusers overcoming, 121–124
Responsibility
    for sexual abuse, 89, 91–92, 148, 181, 221
Resting, 49, 52, 55, 56
Revenge, 146
Re-victimization, 32
Rituals
    and disinhibition, 118
Role-play confrontation, 164–165, 166–167
Running away, 40, 200

S

Safe places
    examples of, 26–27
    imaginary, 24–25
Scratching, 200
Sculpting, 12, 47, 53, 55